FOOL IN LOVE

One Man's Search for Romance
. . . or Something Like It

STEVEN IVORY

A TOUCHSTONE BOOK
Published by Simon & Schuster
New York   London   Toronto   Sydney

TOUCHSTONE
Rockefeller Center
1230 Avenue of the Americas
New York, NY 10020

TOUCHSTONE and colophon are registered trademarks
of Simon & Schuster, Inc.

For information about special discounts for bulk purchases,
please contact Simon & Schuster Special Sales:
1-800-456-6798 or business@simonandschuster.com

"In Search of a Lie I Found the Truth" was adapted from a piece
published in *Essence* Magazine, March 2001.

A number of the stories here were adapted from columns published from 2000 to 2003 on the Electronic Urban Report
(www.eurweb.com), an online newsletter and site.

Designed by Jaime Putorti

Manufactured in the United States of America

10 9 8 7 6 5 4 3 2 1

Library of Congress Cataloging-in-Publication Data
Ivory, Steven.
     Fool in love : one man's search for romance—or something like
it / Steven Ivory.
         p. cm.
     "A Touchstone book."
     1. Ivory, Steven—Relations with women. 2. Journalists—
United States—Biography. I. Title.

PN4874.I94A3 2003
070.92—dc22
[B]   2003190063

ISBN 0-7432-5217-9

FOR MICHAELA

CONTENTS

CONTENTS

INTRODUCTION

WHEN I TOLD A FRIEND I was writing a book about romance where it concerns me, he replied with an undertone of sarcasm, "Oh, I see—it's going to be a book of *short* stories." Another friend coyly remarked that, from any other writer, such a book would qualify as "a labor of *love,* but . . ." Her voice trailed off as she contemplated whether coming from me this book would actually have anything to do with love.

These heartwarming exhibitions of faith emanate

from friends. When I said there would be thirty-three essays, people got wide-eyed and took a step back, as if they might catch something from a man who has bedded thirty-three women.

Actually, this is not a collection of stories about all the relationships I've ever had in my life. In fact, most of these stories are not about romantic relationships at all, but stories about the Search. The stories are based on actual experiences, but I have changed names and other characteristics.

Everyone writes about love, but the Search gets no love. Yet it's the quest for love that will make a man do strange things. Make him go out in public in way too tight pants. The Search will make him lie like a rug. Cause him to spend his rent money to impress a woman. Infinitely worse, it will make him do things that *other* men insist will work in his Search. There is nothing more pathetic than a man who seeks another man's advice on how to be an individual.

You can learn much about love simply by trying to attain it, and ultimately, you discover crucial things about yourself. You could find out that you love being in love. Or you might find what you were searching for and realize you enjoy the chase more than the capture.

During my own Search for true love, I'll be doggone if I didn't discover that many of the partners I've taken have been somehow connected to places, experiences and people of my past, not the least of whom were my parents, especially my mother. Freud may have made the connection ages ago, but the sheer notion still blows my mind. And that is why there are also stories here about my mother. As I see it, this book would not be complete without my taking an honest and affectionate look at the woman who in so many ways set a subliminal standard for what I seek in a mate.

As decidedly whimsical as some of these stories are, reconstructing them was not always a joyful process. Think of old hurt long and hard enough and the pain becomes fresh. Other times, I wished I could go back and relive it just as I did it the first time. Telling the tale called for an honesty that I found necessary only after I attempted to lie. But the only way for us to conquer our fears is to face them, and one of mine has long been the fear of having my feelings exposed—or worse, of having them open to judgment and ridicule. Lest you assume I say this much in the way a big star whines about the burden of fame yet goes to great lengths to ensure his celebrity, I should say this book was not my idea, but the concept of Simon & Schuster Senior Editor Cherise Grant. She read my weekly nonfiction column at the Electronic Urban Report (EUR) website (www.eurweb.com) and proposed a collection of my (mis)adventures in searching for a relationship.

I've never done anything to this woman. Didn't know her before this project. Indeed, as of this writing, I could not tell you what she looks like if my life depended on it. Yet, she has seen to it that by commissioning such a book, I am virtually guaranteed never to have another date in my life. To her credit, at the outset of our talks, she did mention being called shrewd. She never copped to evil. *Fool* in Love. That title was her idea as well. Along with everything else, I guess now I'm a fool, too.

In all seriousness, I am forever indebted to Ms. Grant and not simply because she chose to publish my work. I am appreciative because she persuaded me to do *this* work. There are stories here I've wanted to forget— which is precisely my reason for telling them.

By the way, the Search (and the saga) continues.

—Steven Ivory, April 2003

PART I

THE LAWS OF LOVE

IT ALL BEGINS WITH A . . .

SHE WAS A good-looking woman. At thirty, she had her stuff together: She had a good job at Hughes Aircraft and a new Volkswagen Rabbit. She was buying the Ladera Heights town house she lived in. She could have taught a naive kid like me, all of twenty-four at the time, a thing or two about life. *And* she could cook.

But as I left her place late that night for the second time in a week, clothes rumpled and passions unrequited, there was something in an otherwise beautiful picture that I simply could not ignore: The girl could not kiss.

The two of us wrestled amorously on her couch for the better part of the evening, and no matter how I approached it, the result was always the same—the instant my lips reached hers, she'd open her mouth so wide that she could have easily administered mouth-to-mouth. I tried sneaking up on her lips, to no avail; whenever hers detected mine in the vicinity, they'd again open up—as if to swallow the bottom half of my face. In the end, both literally and figuratively, I simply could not get past the woman's mouth.

There are certainly bigger disappointments in life than finding someone decent, witty and earnest, who smells good and doesn't embarrass you with the way she dresses, and then discovering she doesn't know how to kiss, but there are hardly more frustrating revelations.

If you are a thinking adult over twenty-five who leads a fairly healthy social life and you don't know how to kiss, then one of three things happened: (1) A true freak of nature, you never in your life dated one single person who could kiss; (2) you simply refused to pay attention; or (3) you're a Resister, one whose mouth defiantly refuses to yield to experience and authority. Either way is a sad situation.

Especially when you consider what this deprived

breed has gone proudly through life passing off as a kiss: dramatic, oral assaults of slobbering and slurping, probing, omnipresent tongues and clumsy teeth on the offense. Or indifferent, feeble, obligatory attempts at affection delivered with the romantic verve of a mannequin. There are those who view kissing as something only to be associated with impending sex. Indeed, there are others who don't like to kiss at all and will tell you as much. Get as far away from these people as possible.

For the faltering marriage there is counseling. For sexoholics there is therapy. Every other relationship-associated dysfunction has some type of aid. There should, therefore, be a school for kissing. Because without the kiss, you've got nothing. I know who would be the perfect teacher for such an educational institution: Shirley Brown. When I was sixteen, Shirley lived five doors down from our house. She was just a year older than I was, but seemed a world wiser. For some reason, most of the girls at school despised her.

Shirley's resounding, innate sexuality—her womanly curves, her insistence—scared the hell out of me. But apparently not enough to deter me from taking a nighttime stroll with her to the nearby State Capitol Historical Building, where, while sitting on the steps under a sexy, starry sky, Shirley gave me my very first kiss. She began by administering calming, lingering pecks on my lips before finally parting them with her wet, warm tongue and deep kissing me into a dizzying, euphoric vortex of passion.

After that night, Shirley and I would talk on the phone, and she'd persuade me to walk down to her house on Saturday evenings and watch TV with her while the aunt who was raising her fixed people's hair in the back of the house, giving us the opportunity to smooch. I'd find the nerve to work my hand up Shirley's skirt, rubbing her thick, hairy, brown legs until I'd reach the top of her thigh, where she'd gently but firmly stop my hand. If she had offered "it" up, then what? As it was, she gave up something sexier and infinitely more valuable: Years before I'd lose my virginity, I'd learn from Shirley that kissing was not an appetizer, but the main course.

Somebody once defined a kiss as something humans do when words are no longer sufficient. I have to agree. There are few things in the universe more powerful than a kiss. The moment you've experienced a great one, you won't settle for anything less.

Thank you, Shirley, wherever you are.

And kisses don't lie. Well, sometimes they do. But what a lie. A lie that no one would blame anyone for ignoring, for just a little while.

EAU DE FEET (AND EVERYTHING ELSE)!

IN 1987, just before Ramon Hervey flew to New York to marry actress/singer Vanessa Williams, he invited me to a bachelor party pitched in his honor one evening at a friend's house in Los Angeles.

By the way, someone really should give this thing another title.

"Bachelor party" sounds like a set of randy college kids toasting a guy's final night as a single man one last time before he takes the hand of a girl named Becky. In fact, every bachelor party I've attended was simply a reason for grown men to behave like rambunctious, frisky teenagers. The attendees hope the guy finds happiness and all, but it's really about the strippers, and the three females for hire at Hervey's send-off were in the middle of a no-holds-barred performance when comedian/actor Franklin Ajaye spoke up.

It wasn't enough that these women, writhing through configurations only a gynecologist could respect, were already nearly as naked as the day they were born; Ajaye requested they lose the scuffed white pumps. "I wanna see some feet!" he and a couple other guys taunted playfully. I sat mute in silent hope.

We humans are strange creatures, driven by various peculiarities that climb into our subconscious early in life and make themselves at home. Most people, whether or not they are conscious of this, have something that floats their boat.

Myself, I'm a foot man.

I'm not obsessive about it. Not interested in eating a meal off a woman's feet or having her walk across my face. However, a pair of good-looking well-maintained feet, plain or sporting a deluxe pedicure, will always get my attention. It would be great if said feet were attached to a pleasant, emotionally adjusted, smart and witty woman, but truth be told, pretty feet would allow me to look past the apparent inadequacies of the Wicked Witch of the West. For a little while, anyway.

To somebody into elbows or women who smoke cigarettes while eating Mexican food on Tuesdays, my thing sounds unusual. Alas, as Diana Ross moaned during "Love Hangover," if there's a cure for this, I don't want it. Besides, I firmly believe that if we were all honest about our fixations—as long as they are pursued between consenting adults, no one is hurt and no property destroyed—the world would be a less stressful place.

For many, the origin of a certain sensual craving is inexplicable, but I know distinctly when and where I developed mine. I was in kindergarten. My teacher, Miss Garner, my first teacher's crush, had us unfold our mats on the floor for the after-lunch nap. I loved Miss Garner and stuck close to her when I could. I ended up camped near her desk. She sat in silence, reading *The Daily Oklahoman* and munching on cafeteria butter cookies, and had slipped out of her shoes to reveal her stocking feet.

I was startled. At age four, I didn't know teachers even had feet. But there Miss Garner's were, little more than arm's length away, motionless but for the occasional twitch of a toe.

I lay entranced in covert observation, fascinated by the sight of a woman's feet, confounded by my sudden light-headedness and the knot forming in the pit of my stomach. Then came the utterly strange sensation that I now know was the first erection that I can remember.

On a certain day at a certain moment, an emotional/sexual sensation can be sparked by any number of experiences. Obviously, I'd seen women's feet before in my young life, but my crush transformed an ordinary occurrence into a seminal moment of sexuality.

During the humid summers of my adolescence, I discreetly paid special attention to barefoot neighborhood girls who went past our house to Butler's Bar-B-Q or Washington Park, seeking relief for tender soles from the hot sidewalk in whatever cool, green grass lay along the route. I wouldn't truly make a sexual connection to my curiosity about women's feet until adulthood.

I am hardly alone in my penchant. It's just that leg, butt and breast aficionados have openly had their desires satiated, while the foot man has languished in the shadows. More respect has been given to men who are into high-heeled women. What deviant mind invites a woman to bed in shoes?

Things have come around for the foot man, though. Television commercials that have absolutely nothing to do with feet will feature a woman showing hers off. Entertainers and models pose for magazine and CD covers with their feet strategically positioned to enhance the

10

shot. Since these images seldom feature ugly feet, you have to believe all this is done consciously.

Pedicures, once optional, became commonplace years ago; toe rings and anklets are familiar even among the most conservative dressers.

But I am the last one to talk a woman out of the choices she makes in her personal notion of sexuality, especially when I consider the vast lists of utterly stupid things men do to impress women, and the years it took me to be honest about my own interests.

Marvin Jenkins was the first guy I met who made no bones about his interest in women's feet. Marvin fascinated and embarrassed me with frank, expert discussion about arches, shoes danglers, and his preference for thick ankles.

One time he and several friends, myself included, engaged in a lively game of bid whist at the apartment he shared with his beautiful wife, Toni. The two had had words because Marvin decided to hang with us although he and Toni had committed to attending a birthday party.

Toni opted to go alone, and when she finally emerged from their bedroom, a crony who knew Marvin's preferences mumbled something about his actually letting his wife go out "dressed like that." The uninitiated would find nothing provocative about a flowered Laura Ashley–type number that literally covered her from the neck to just above her ankles. Her footwear, however, was another story.

Toni had slid her small, pedicured and painted feet, adorned with a silver anklet and toe ring, into a pair of wooden, flip-flop-styled Dr. Scholl's sandals. As she smugly made her way across the room for the front door, every flap of that bleached Dr. Scholl's wood against her soft, lotioned soles was like a slap upside Marvin's head. After she left, Marvin was never quite the same. His mind was on his woman's feet—feet that could attract some other guy with Marvin's particular preoccupation.

If Dana was aware I was interested in her feet, she never let on. Not that she would have asked, and not that I would have mentioned it. But she kept her feet covered for so long that I began to fear what I might find. My inexact science—she had little hands with a small fingernail bed—indicated she had pretty feet, but I couldn't be sure.

When she finally displayed them in open-toed Manolo Blahniks at Mirabelle's during an after-work drink, my first thought was that it is a good thing wings are an angel's primary mode of travel, for somewhere in heaven was one without feet.

Her toenails were resplendent in pink polish and well proportioned to the rest of her feet, which exhib-

ited a perfect, not too high arch and not too skinny ankles. I felt a rush. Damn you, Miss Garner.

Dana noticed that I took more than a passing interest
and met my generous compliment with a congenial but
firm admonishment: She'd briefly dated a kooky guy
who was obsessed with her feet to the point it made her
uncomfortable. "I don't want nobody messing with my
feet," she scoffed.

I laughed and assured her that neither she nor her
feet would have problems with me.

And she didn't. When, the following weekend, she
kicked off her Donna Karan sandals on our blanket in a
secluded area of Will Rogers Park, I was cool. When
cuddling led to petting and kissing, the mere idea that I
was in the company of a woman who performed Tom
Jones's "It's Not Unusual" at karaoke with gleeful abandon was enough.

But then Dana unbuttoned my shirt and with impassioned deliberation began a trail with her tongue over
my right breast, giving brief attention to the nipple before making her way first up to my shoulder and then to
my upper bicep. My intrigue degenerated into puzzle-
ment, when Dana paused at my armpit the way a vam-
pire, its mouth watering and fangs at the ready, hesitates
for dramatic effect at the nape of its victim's neck before
digging in.

The mild-mannered Dana, who had reprimanded me for even looking at her feet, was an armpit freak!

With her hazel eyes rolled back in her head, Dana seemed to be in a trance as she fed deliriously on the pit of my arm like a greedy animal at a trough. She wrapped her legs around my right thigh and slowly writhed in hungry desperation.

As I fought physical discomfort and the urge to snicker from being ticklish, I looked down past Dana's gyrating, blue-jeaned buttocks, past her alternately curling and spreading toes, to see in the distance a park ranger working his index finger together in a tsk-tsk motion and silently mouthing to me, "No sex in the park"—to which I wanted to reply, "But we're not having sex here," a communiqué interrupted by Dana's muffled but boisterous orgasm. Well, I guess one of us isn't, anyway.

Dana finally emerged from my right armpit, her face wearing a look of embarrassment and glazed with remnants of unscented Dry Idea. She chuckled sheepishly and said she didn't know what came over her. I joked that *she* was what came over me. Still in a postorgasm haze, she didn't get it.

During the drive back to Los Angeles she admitted having a lifelong appetite for certain male armpits, sparked, she deduced, when she was a child and the handsome friend of her older brother put her in a head-lock. She was lucky enough to live once with a mate who indulged her fetish, but after being ridiculed by a subsequent lover, she abandoned her interest. I'd not been in the presence of *this* Dana—tranquil, laid-back, emotionally forthcoming, equipped with a pair of gorgeous feet and, so it seemed, a yen for the sweaty pit of a man's arm. This could work.

I knew it wouldn't, however, when I heard the tone of Dana's voice on my machine the next morning and realized she was back to her meticulously uptight self. When I picked up, she apologized profusely for the "incident" in the park, adding that she was too busy with work to be involved in something full-time.

I ribbed her that perhaps this was really about my brand of deodorant. Then I told her that I appreciated her being comfortable enough with me to let go and that it endeared her to me even more. Silence.

She was going to lose me, she said, as she was driving into her company's underground parking lot. She wrapped up our conversation the way she'd close a deal on a property, and then she was gone. We discussed it all again a day later, for naught. Getting exactly what you want usually relieves tension, but apparently, my armpits weren't enough for Dana, whose reluctance to follow her deep desires left us both wanting more.

HOW TO MAKE
LEMON PIE

OH, LORD," Stewart James sarcastically groaned one morning from the steps of Los Angeles City College's radio broadcasting department. "Check out Royce."

That was his name, but we called him Styles in affectionate honor of his rather eccentric threads. From Charlotte, North Carolina, by way of Harlem, Styles had the hip-ology of Sammy Davis, Jr., the raucous wit and vaguely effeminate tendencies of Little Richard and, at thirty-something in 1973, perhaps fifteen years on his average classmate.

I figured his seniority and a stint in the military to be the sources of the industrial-strength audacity that allowed a man to stroll in public alternately dressed as if he'd stepped off a Vegas stage or out of a blaxploitation flick. However, today's fluorescent lime green bell-bottomed jumpsuit was too much even for Styles.

Then again, this was the first man I'd ever seen in person— meaning not on TV or in a movie—wear an ascot. At junior college, no less.

His fashion choices may have set some of our classmates off balance, but I dug Styles. Underneath the three-piece sharkskin suits and floor-length pleather coats lived a warm soul with a sharp tongue whose verve entranced me. "Forget lemonade—I'm making lemon meringue pie, baby!" was typical of Styles's outlook on life.

One day during lunch at the campus snack bar, Styles and I took the last chairs at an outdoor table occupied by two Casanovas desperately seeking to impress a twenty-something beauty in Afro puffs and, to my nervous delight, "Armenian Girl," whom I didn't know but had flirted with during the semester.

Armenian Girl's eyes smiled at me, while one guy went on about his car and daddy's money. I was relieved that Styles remained uncharacteristically silent while tending to his egg salad sandwich. My relief was short-lived.

"You like seafood?" he blurted to Miss Afro Puffs, bringing the table to a screeching halt. " 'Cause I know a private place in Malibu that has great seafood. My man here and me goin' tomorrow night. You ladies care to join us?"

One of the playboys cut Styles a menacing glare, took notice of the cocked black "apple" cap and black-and-white polka-dot tie and issued a mocking snicker that said, "You gotta be kidding."

But sure enough, the following evening, Styles's wine-colored Seville cruised up the Pacific Coast Highway deep into Malibu, a gray Volkswagen bug carrying my girl Adelina and her friend Vonetta faithfully trailing behind. I kept one eye in the side-view mirror, astonished and gleeful at my luck, until I realized that my weak wallet had been committed to a fancy seafood dinner.

"I gotcha covered, baby," Styles said calmly. "But your girl Armour Star was sittin' there makin' all kinda eyes at you and you were gonna let those bourgie cats take her. Whatever it is, you have to go for what you want in life, Ivory. Especially if it's just sitting there." Styles made sense. His shirt didn't; not with that sweater. His words, however, rang true.

Soon, Styles rolled down his window and motioned for our dates to make a U-turn onto the road's shoulder, where the sun was setting on a desolate stretch of beach, no restaurant in sight.

"What's wrong?" I asked.

"We here," said Styles, opening his door.

"Styles, man, don't do this to me." I felt like crying.

"Listen, we got these chicks here now. So get on out."

The shy Adelina appeared bewildered, but Vonetta was unquestionably pissed—no motherfuckin' restaurant?—until Styles opened his trunk to reveal a virtual feast of assorted goodies. There were torches, blankets, the requisite checkered tablecloth and, wading in a huge pot of water, four live lobsters awaiting their fate.

Several hours, two bottles of wine and a sumptuous meal later, with torches aflame and Stevie Wonder's "Superwoman" on the portable stereo, the three of us raised our glasses to our host.

With Adelina under the stars and a blanket in Malibu, it felt like love. We sat cheek to cheek and talked about all kinds of things as I watched Styles work his magic. "I knew I could show you something you've never seen before," he said coyly to a mellow Vonetta as he refreshed her glass.

"Honey, I've seen the ocean before," she said.

"Ocean?" retorted Styles with ample cool. "I'm talkin' 'bout my sweater—one hundred fit-tee percent pure cashmere, baby."

In one swoop of ingenuity, not only did Styles feed us

royally and jump-start my romance with Adelina, he illustrated to me a valuable life lesson. As he'd say
throughout our college friendship, it's not the lemons—
the situation at hand—but what you do with them.

Of course, it was Adelina's father, an old hard-liner
from the Armenian Republic, who would later con-
tribute a brusque addendum to Styles's gospel.

A short, solemn Russian tank in a wife-beater, he sat
between Adelina and me on the couch, gazing at the
television when I called on her at home in Glendale. He
spoke hardly a syllable of English, but when he said it
was time for me to go, I understood completely. I shook
both their hands, never to return. Dad's lesson: Women
are not lemons, Styles. Not his daughter, anyway.

FINNY AND ME

WE MET AT THE Rose Cafe in Venice. Not Venice, Italy, but Venice, California, the arty little community next to Santa Monica.

On the weekends, especially late Sunday mornings, it can be difficult to get a seat at the Rose. The unpretentious restaurant, with its healthy menu of assorted salads, soups, breads and desserts, is a tasty magnet for local artists, writers, runners, skaters, bodybuilders and upscale weekenders from surrounding areas. Sometimes, by the time you order your food at the counter and get through the register line, the table you were eyeing is gone.

That's what happened to the lean, striking brown woman who stood before me with a tray in her hand. She was five foot seven, fashionably bohemian, wearing a tiny, frayed T-shirt, an ankle-length peach skirt and sandals revealing matching peach painted toes. Handmade beads and jewelry adorned her neck and wrists.

I noticed her when she walked in. Our eyes met briefly, but hers instantly danced away, as if she was shy or didn't want to be bothered. All that changed the moment she needed a place to sit and realized my table was all that was available.

"I guess the gods say I am to sit with you," she said, with detached sweetness in an accent that sounded Portuguese.

We made uneasy small talk that got easier as it went. She was a twenty-seven-year-old Virgo, ten years my junior. She said she was single, though more than once her conversation painted the picture of a partner.

That funky jewelry was her own creation, which she sold to several L.A.-area retail stores. While toying with one of her long black pigtails, she spoke of being the only child of a Cuban mother who once sang professionally in Havana and a Portuguese father who worked here for the government of Brazil, where she'd spent her adolescence. Long after chicken salad, lentil soup and bowtie pasta, we were still sitting there chatting about music and the continued pollution of the ocean and the air, long enough to share a slice of Rose's bread pudding before taking a stroll to the boardwalk.

I found it remarkable that a person could seem aloof one minute and so warm and funny the next. At the end of a day that took us both by surprise, we exchanged numbers and agreed to see each other again.

And we did. Over the ensuing weeks we met in Beverly Hills for drinks, hit greasy spoons downtown for lunch and had dinner in Santa Monica. I liked her. I was charmed by that Brazilian accent and her quirky, creative persona. There was a certain innocence, which I found sexy. She was a bit self-possessed, and perhaps just this side of nutty, which only enhanced her allure. After all, as she'd gallantly remind me, "I am an artiste!"

However, I remained perplexed by how often she used the word "we" when mentioning home life, as in "Yes, we love the rain in the fall," or "We overslept this morning." There wasn't a roommate; she'd voiced disdain for the mere concept. I blamed the plural reference on her sporadic struggle with English.

But in the weeks we'd known each other, she'd never allowed me to pick her up, saying Los Feliz, where she lived, was too far a drive from my West Hollywood apartment, and she preferred to steer her tan, beat-up '60s Rambler to wherever we decided to meet. Despite her generally congenial way, there seemed to be a wall. She was happy one minute, then intense and indifferent the next.

One evening she called me from her parents' home in Santa Monica, where she had just finished dinner. "They were going to drive me home, but if you had the time," she said teasingly, "I'd treat you to dessert at the Ivy and then you could drive me home." Since meeting her at the Rose, I'd become as smitten as a schoolboy. I got on the freeway and fantasized that the word "dessert" must have a double entendre in Brazil.

She asked me to wait in the car since she'd rather come right out, but apparently the plan didn't appeal to her curious father, who held his little girl's hand as he accompanied her down the driveway. He was small but sturdy, reminding me of Latin jazz percussionist Willie Bobo and actor Anthony Quinn. She was wearing jeans, clogs and a faded red T-shirt with a yellow hammer, sickle and star logo of the old Communist Party. In the distance, behind the screen door of their neat classic clapboard house, a slight woman stood observing with her hands on her hips. I could hear a little dog yapping like crazy.

I got out of the car, and Willie Quinn smiled warmly as he submitted me to a once-over and a handshake that momentarily stopped the circulation in my left hand. He kissed his daughter, spoke to her in his native tongue and after the three of us stood there for a minute or two admiring the beautiful sunset, I walked her around to the passenger side of the car and she got in.

After carrot cake and tea at the Ivy, during the ride to her apartment, she drifted between preoccupation and giddiness.

"Father likes you," she said, smiling.

"How do you know?" I asked. "Better yet, how does he know?"

"He said so. In Portuguese. My father is a very wise man."

"Then he also knows that I like his daughter."

"They are surprised. I don't like many men."

"Then I'm lucky."

"No. Not yet."

I pulled over in front of an old Spanish-style fourplex. I kept the engine running so she wouldn't think I was focused only on prolonging the evening. When she requested I turn the car off, I was happy I'd hopped into the shower before coming down here. "I want you to meet someone," she said thoughtfully, sitting there, looking straight ahead. Okay—when? "Now. Come up with me."

The high ceilings and books and old black-and-white photographs and classic pieces of worn, beautiful furniture gave it the cluttered grace typical of the abode of a creative mind. It was no surprise that a huge, framed portrait of Mexican painter Frida Kahlo, whose colorful, turbulent personal life contributed as much, if not more, to her legend as her paintings, adorned a wall. Small boxes of assorted beads and ornaments lay scattered on a huge wooden dining table. This was also headquarters for her fledgling jewelry business.

She cleared the couch of magazines and newspapers so that we could sit, kicked off her clogs, reached over to a boom box to find a classical music station and asked if I wanted to split a can of guava juice.

"Who is it you want me to meet?" I delicately pressed. The anticipation was beginning to wear on me. I hoped this wasn't some ol' freaky shit involving another dude or something. And I wasn't in the mood for communicating with spirits or entertaining any other equally off-the-wall indulgence this girl was just peculiar enough to suggest. I was gently playing with her hand when she said, "Bem, meu caro pequeño gato! We are pleased that you could join us!"

Standing in the doorway that connected the living room to the hallway and staring at me with the intensity of a deer caught in headlights was a cat. If you are a lover of cats, you'd probably say that this cat was a beautiful Siamese of perfect weight and length with unique markings. Since I could take or leave cats, I simply saw a cat— whose seemingly conceited attitude was magnified by its sparkling, jewel-like collar.

She continued to coo praises to the animal, which, initially standing, now sat, balled up as cats do when they sit on somebody's porch or the hood of a car, its penetrating eyes still on me. Finally, it sauntered into the middle of the living room and, with its back to us, stretched, as if giving us the opportunity to adore it.

"This is who I wanted you to meet," she said, taking the cat up in her arms and bringing it to the couch. Since I was half expecting a woman, child or muscular, tattooed guy with a lisp saying, "Let's party," I was relieved.

Two years earlier, a disintegrating relationship had left her so aggrieved that she did nothing but sleep. Her mother suggested therapy. Instead, her father surprised her with a kitten from the litter of a cat belonging to a friend at the Brazilian consulate. "This cat gave me something to live for," she said rather dramatically. The two became inseparable. The tiny Siamese was impassive to most people, disdained all brand X cat food and refused to do its business on just any old kitty litter. So she christened it Finnicka.

"This is my sister, my guardian and the love of my life," she proudly declared. "But it has been just the two of us for too long. We are ready to add someone to our lives." She was silent. Then: "To be honest, she does not much care for men. That she sits in my lap with you next to me . . . this is very good."

As she gently stroked the cat's back, I reached over to put my hand on hers; it seemed the thing to do in honor of a defining moment. But my affection was met by a left paw that, with the lightning swiftness of a young Muhammad Ali, rose up and connected. If I hadn't felt the sting and seen the blood, I would not have believed it happened. "Oh, this is just a love tap," she surmised. "This is her way of getting acquainted. She would not be this close if she was not willing to like you."

BETWEEN CERTAIN WOMEN and the feline species seems to exist an interdependence that most men will never fully grasp. Cats may be moody, but so are many women; inherently, they understand one another. When the woman ahead of you in the grocery checkout line loads enough cat food to last a nuclear winter onto the conveyor belt, she is saying that, while she may love men—and may even have one—she doesn't need one; she's got a devoted cat (or two or five) who listens to

her, won't cheat and doesn't insist on holding the TV remote.

However, best I can tell, the cat is no substitute for a
man, nor is it meant to be. I imagine their relationship
to be a lot like that of women who take the occasional female lover but wouldn't consider themselves lesbians.
Women have told me this doesn't have as much to do
with sex as it is a kind of genderless camaraderie they
often cannot experience with a man.

This is not to say a woman and her cats always get
along. Cats pout, deliberately stay away from home for
days at a time to spite their owners over disagreements,
and exhibit other behavior traits normally synonymous
with human beings. At least this is what the women say,
and if a man interested in a woman who owns cats is
smart, he'll keep his mouth shut and not dispute any of
this. I, for one, thought the idea of a cat having a clear
and distinct personality was bullshit. Then I met
Finnicka.

A WEEK AFTER first visiting her apartment, I picked up
the new apple of my eye for dinner and a movie. During
the evening, I noticed that my introduction to the cat
seemed to free her, that our time together was devoid of
the previous tension and mood swings. Indeed, when I
drove her home after a nightcap at the Peninsula, she

invited me in. Finnicka took one look at her guest and grudgingly departed the living room. However, when I opened my eyes in the throes of our impassioned couch make-out, there was the cat sitting in the middle of the room, staring in disgust as the hand she'd scratched the hell out of a couple days earlier fondled her mistress's left breast. When my friend excused herself to take a quick shower, Finnicka escorted her to the bathroom door, but in a minute was again sitting in the middle of the living room eyeing me, possibly to ensure that I didn't steal anything. I thought it the perfect occasion for us to have a chat.

"Hi."

She began to clean herself.

Who knows what, in this woman's tea or perfume, encouraged me to initiate dialogue with a cat. Perhaps it had to do with her mentioning the animal in nearly every one of our conversations of late—and thus the sneaking suspicion that the future of our relationship rested in Finnicka's snobby paws.

"You know," I began, "we have something in common. We both like her very much. I know you feel your job is to take care of her, to see that she isn't hurt. After all, you two have been together for a while now. But I'm not here to hurt, and I don't want to be hurt. And by no means am I here to try and replace you. I'd like us to be friends."

Finnicka stopped licking and gazed up into my face. The tone of my voice, if not my words, seemed to be having a favorable impact. Then she cast her eyes upon my feet as if to say, "Your shoes are hideous," and scurried away.

I'm not a big fan of homogenized sax music. But when you're slightly intoxicated, horny, naked and in bed under scented sheets with a beautiful woman whose eccentricity suggests she could be quite uninhibited if put at ease, Bony James and Kenny G can resonate like the music of angels.

In the shadow of flickering candles, I couldn't help but notice Finnicka sitting smugly in the bedroom doorway at first, and then suddenly at my foot on top of the bed. "She's probably just sleepy," said my lover. Would-be lover. Nothing had happened yet. Then why doesn't she go to sleep?

"Because you are in her spot. She sleeps with me."

The night was long. There was affection, but no sex. I blamed the cat for this. The cat, meanwhile, undoubtedly blamed me for not getting any sleep. I figured we were even, until morning, when, wafting from the living room came the reprimand, "Oh, Finnicka, What will I do with you?" Still in bed, I was served a breakfast of Danish, half a mango, hot mint tea and the bulletin that my shirt—the brand-new, white button-down with cuffs that I'd just worn for the first time—had been peed on. "This could mean she is claiming you for her own, no?" my guest said mischievously.

I looked at her, hoping this was an attempt at humor. This cat peed on my shirt. Alfred Hitchcock could have made this cat a star. It was time to admit to myself that the cat was going to be a problem.

I thought I was alone in my daft view of Finnicka—or "Finny," as her owner often annoyingly referred to the beast—until a couple of days later, when we decided to meet for lunch. Since she was already in Santa Monica at her parents', we decided to rendezvous in that town, at the Old King's Head, for fish and chips. Her father answered the phone. After exchanging pleasantries, his voice dropped to a murmur, as if, looking over his shoulder, he was about to disclose the classified secrets of a foreign government.

"How are you getting along with the cat?" he asked urgently.

"The cat?"

"The cat. Finnicky."

"She's quite a cat," I said.

"My friend, you can be honest with me."

"Well, it's been—"

"Listen," he interrupted, in hushed, almost apologetic exasperation, choosing not to wait for what he

probably knew was going to be a bullshit answer anyway. "I only gave her this cat to make her happy. Now
the cat does not like *me!* This is unnatural, my friend. If
you can get past this creature, you will have achieved
something. . . ." He attempted to temper the gravity of
his words with an uneasy laugh, then: "VINDO! TELE-
PHONE! Forgive me, my friend. Good luck to you."

ONE SATURDAY AFTERNOON during the unstable courtship
of my Portuguese love, we decided to take a walk
through Griffith Park and stopped at her place first so
she could change her footwear. Heading for her bedroom closet, she warned me to be mindful of the front
door, as the cat "will surely flee." At which point I imagined this door having no hinges.

"Go, my friend," I said to my nemesis, sitting there
licking its paws.

"Now is your chance. You're free."

The cat looked up into my face and then at the open
door, a tantalizing summer breeze blowing through its
whiskers.

"Look! A big, wide world awaits you. Fresh air. Trees
to climb. Birds to chase. Go! But watch out for the cars
on the streets—tires don't relent to sharp claws like my
flesh did when you laid into me. And since we really
can't be certain that you've got eight more lives ahead of

the miserable existence you currently lead, do be careful. But please do go. Adios, you evil, cock-blocking witch."

The cat didn't budge, thank God. If it had, I'd have been history—my crazy artiste would have sunk back into her loveless coma and her father would have had me alternately canonized and strangled. It was a heady thought while it lasted, though.

"You know," I said, closing the door and taking a seat on the couch, "you would not have lasted very long in my neighborhood as a child. I'd have caught you in the alley one day. Or Donny would have."

"I wouldn't be in an alley, you moron," Finnicka replied. "Alleys are for alley cats, and I am Siamese."

"Oh, yeah, you'd be in the alley. You're a cat, and cats love alleys. You'd know that, if you didn't stay cooped up in here gawking at my every move. Of course you'd be in the alley. You think you're different from any other cat because of that collar around your neck? Those aren't real jewels, sister. They're just plastic beads. She made that over there on the table."

Silence.

"Tell me something," I said. "What did I ever do to you?"

"You're vulgar and you're cheap," Finnicka scoffed.

"Cheap? How am I cheap?"

"You're just like all the others who traipse in here, try

to say the right things to get what they want and then leave."

"Did she say I was cheap?"

"In fact, you're worse than the others, because, in addition to everything else, you are an idiot."

"Why am I an idiot?"

"'Because you are having a conversation with a cat."

"No, I'm not."

"Yes, you are. Your mouth is moving. You're looking at me. That's a conversation."

"I'm just trying to reason with you."

"Don't try to reason with me. You're vulgar, you're cheap and you're an idiot, and I want you to stop talking to me."

"Did you say something?" asked my date, standing there in her Nikes. I told her I was imagining a conversation with her cat. She laughed and said I was silly. Silly was a step up from cheap, vulgar idiot.

SHE OPENED HER APARTMENT door wearing a festive mask and not much else, laughing hysterically and waving a Polaroid picture in my face. Her breath reeked of wine. I was there this evening, having answered a handmade invitation that arrived in the mail a week earlier, touting an intimate party for two, her version of the Brazilian Mardi Gras. As the invitation emphasized "underwear optional," I imagined this evening could be particularly adventurous. I also knew a certain cat would be lying in wait to foil the festivities.

To be fair, while I knew Finnicka wasn't entirely innocent, I also knew her owner's maniacal attachment to her was as much the problem as the cat's innate territorial ways. My mission was clear: find a way to sensitively defuse my four-legged adversary while rekindling her mistress's faith in mankind. And achieve all this without the support of underwear.

"Isn't it the cutest thing you've ever seen?" she said, presenting a snapshot of evil incarnate in a party hat. "I couldn't get her to wear it longer than it took to get the picture. Hey! Cat in the hat! Get it?" A terrible dishonor to the memory of Dr. Seuss. I headed for her kitchen, navigating through a living room decorated with purple, yellow and green balloons and streamers, and had to laugh. Her big, joyful approach to life was what I loved about the girl. The aroma of Brazilian cuisine simmering on the stove was an added delight.

I took a bottle of Dom Pérignon out of the paper bag and, just in case domestic animals truly can read, made sure the label was visible to that nosy cat, peering contemptuously from the top of the refrigerator.

Then I placed on the kitchen table a package wrapped in nondescript white paper and, against the raucous sound of Brazilian carnival music blaring from the living room, carefully, methodically unfurled it until the three of us gazed in wonder at its contents: a thick, gorgeous pink slice of salmon.

"There was no need to bring food," said my guest, clearly peeved. "We have plenty."

"It's not for us," I replied. "It's for Finnicka."

That I figured the cat into the evening pleasantly overwhelmed her.

Unfortunately, whether my move would have the desired effect wasn't up to her. But then, what cat couldn't dig a fresh cut of fish? Cooed into confused excitement by her mistress, Finnicka jumped from the fridge, onto the counter and then to the floor, looking up at the table with an expression totally out of her snotty character. Suddenly, costume jewelry collar not withstanding, she was just a cat craving a taste of something she'd missed all her stuck-up little life.

I broke off a small piece of fish and bent down to offer it. She backed away at first. In a second, however, her palpitating nostrils betrayed her, and the beast cautiously eased its face into my palm. She took a small bite, another and then gorged as if she had not eaten in days. The lady of the house was elated and, perhaps, just a little envious as my archenemy ate right out of my hand. Game over.

Later on, my beautiful hostess and I feasted on homemade chicken Stroganoff, softshell crabs in coconut milk, plantains, Brazilian-style collard greens, feijoada and a leafy salad. For dessert we had passion fruit mousse, Brazilian brownies and Brazilian-style banana pie. And for Finnicka, there was fresh salmon—as much as I could personally stuff into her silver dish in the kitchen.

There would be no jazz-from-concentrate that night; this time, Jobim's romantic bossa nova was the impassioned music to which the flickering flames of candles would dance. We lay in bed, bathing in the shadows they cast, my Brazilian love on my left and Finnicka, nestled to my right, purring lovingly in my ear and passing gas like a truck driver, the unlikely fragrance of our new friendship.

BLIND DATE

JANICE AND MARTY said they had "just the girl" for me.

I wish I had a dime for every time someone has told me this. I wouldn't be rich, but I'd have enough change in my pockets to know that certain friends and associates (particularly couples) consider me to be a lonely so-and-so for whom time is rapidly running out.

It is also one of the easiest ways, when you finally meet that date, to get your feelings hurt: *This* woman, who speaks mostly in slang, pops Juicy Fruit incessantly and refers to shrimp as "scrimps"—*this* is how you see me? *This* is what I inspire?

A perennially single buddy of mine likes to call the hookup by emissary a "referral." The kind of person you get set up with depends on the gender doing the setting up: Generally, when a woman recommends someone to you, the emphasis will be on the cerebral. Who the prospect is as a person will be far more important than her looks. More than likely, she'll be able to cook. When a man recommends a date, she'll be physically equipped in a way "that I know you're gonna like." She's probably someone he'd personally like to indulge intimately, but can't for some innocuous technicality like she happens to be the best friend of his girlfriend or his sister-in-law. When a couple fixes you up, on the other hand, it's as if your credit has been approved. After all, this is a couple—you figure they know a little more about who will work with whom.

After weeks of begging off the idea, I conceded to Janice and Marty and agreed to phone their friend. She said Marsha, herself apprehensive about being set up, for safety's sake, would rather call me, which she did one Saturday afternoon. The voice oozing through the receiver was pleasantly assured and rather flirtatious. We hadn't talked very long when suddenly she said, "Hey! How spontaneous are you?"

"Let me guess—you want to meet."

"Right now."

"You're kidding. Right now?"

"Why not? I've known Janice and Marty for twenty years," she chirped. "I don't think they'd introduce me to a mass murderer. This way, we can be done with this. Who knows? We might actually like each other."

She chose a restaurant situated between the two of us. We described ourselves and what we'd be wearing, and agreed to meet at the bar in an hour. She sounded sane enough. To use her words, who knows? We might actually like each other. I was intrigued.

I parked my car in the restaurant lot and was headed across it toward the place when I tripped. My shoe connected with one of those concrete blocks in parking lots that keep cars from rolling too far forward. My attempt to avoid going down failed, and I prepared myself to hit the pavement.

I must have put my hands out to soften my collision with the blacktop, but I don't remember doing that. Nor do I recall hitting the ground.

I just remember coming to on my back after being out for what felt like thirty minutes, but was probably more like thirty or forty seconds. It's amazing how relaxed momentary unconsciousness can leave you. Even before opening my eyes, I heard the sound of people scurrying toward me.

"Wow, that guy just passed out over there," said a voice in the distance.

"Oh my God," someone else remarked.

I wanted to correct them—I didn't pass out; I tripped and must have hit my head when I fell. Besides a slight headache, I didn't feel any pain. Everything seemed to be in working order, but I couldn't be entirely sure because, at least for the moment, I dare not move a limb. I was paralyzed—with embarrassment.

What sounded like a family of three stood over me, anxiously pondering my predicament. I discerned their number by hearing the urgent voice of a young girl, maybe barely in her teens, saying, "Dad! Go call 9-1-1!"

As he ran away, the girl then said, "Mom, do we have something in the car to put under his head?" The sound of yet another person rushing off. Wow, I thought, this little girl is bright; she's in control. I thought it odd that her parents, whoever they were, would comply with their daughter's orders and leave her holding vigil over a dying man, but I was appreciative of their little operation on my behalf.

In fact, I was beginning to feel a little shitty about the whole thing. These folks were giving their all to someone they didn't know from Adam sprawled in a restaurant parking lot, and I didn't have the guts to get my ass up from here, go on about my business and let them get on with theirs. While a couple of bystanders whispered among themselves, the young girl gently pressed my wrist with her index finger.

Awww, how sweet, I thought. I wanted to explain to her that you have to feel the inside of the wrist to read a pulse, but her presence felt so intensely earnest that surely I'd scare her to death if I suddenly spoke up. When I "come to," I thought, I'm going to thank this family for all their help—and for raising such a dynamic young lady. She was so concerned and so . . . Aar-rrrrrrrgh! ! What the. . . ? !

Apparently, when the little girl didn't detect a pulse, she decided to take matters into her own hands—hands that were now placed squarely on my chest and pumping away—and in the valiant process, damn near caved my chest in. I didn't know if a perfectly healthy person had ever died from CPR, but this chick was about to kill me. I needed to show some signs of life, and fast. I began to cough and slowly "regain" consciousness. The last part was an act. The coughing was real.

"He's waking up!" the girl triumphantly declared.

"Praise God!" someone said. Slowly, I opened my eyes to find a little blond girl on her knees and staring into my face with the utmost concern.

"Don't get up," said the father, who resembled the

talk-show host Phil Donahue, only not as gray-haired. I began to thank him and his daughter, but he interrupted me. "We have to take care of one another," he said, against a siren in the distance, adding, "I called the paramedics." Oh my God. I'd seen those guys work before. They undo your clothes, expose your underwear right there on the street. I had to get out of here, but I had to pace myself—shake my grogginess at an authentic rate.

Discreetly, I eyed my audience—the handful of people who were content to let my new adopted family do all the work. People are a trip, I thought. Standing there, gawking as if they were at the zoo. Look at the guy with the Hawaiian shirt, nonchalantly licking an ice cream cone as if this were a carnival and I were the featured attraction. There's a small boy holding the hand of his father, gaping as if he'd seen a ghost. Man, don't have your poor son out here looking at a man suffering from embarrassment on the street; you'll traumatize him for life.

And how about that attractive woman peering over the shoulders of those two senior citizens. You'd think she had better things to do than . . . wait a minute—purple top, braids, about five foot five . . . that's . . . my date! This was the woman I'd come to meet, staring at a man napping on the pavement who fit the description of her blind rendezvous.

Our eyes connected, and immediately she knew I knew . . . that she knew. At that instant I was distracted by the paramedics arriving with siren blaring and lights flashing. When I looked back around, she was gone. Gone before I could say, "Heeey, how ya doin'? . . . Look, there's nothing wrong with me; I'm as healthy as an ox. I'm not on crack or anything . . . I've never even tried crack; wouldn't know what it looked like . . . I was—ha, this is *so* funny—I was simply so excited about the possibility that behind the phone wit and playfulness could be someone that resembled, well, *you,* that I tripped over myself, uh, I mean, over one of those things there that keep cars from rolling forward. . . ."

The thought of her briskly heading back to her car, no doubt disappointed by all this, sent my condition from mere embarrassment to decomposition. I wondered if the ambulance had a straitjacket on board. Or a casket. I've officially been embarrassed to death. Just take me straight to the nearest cemetery and put me in the ground, why don't you.

I attempted to soothe my ego by asking myself just what kind of woman would leave her potential husband decaying in a restaurant parking lot without the common decency of introducing herself or inquiring as to what had happened. The answer came crashing back onto my chest harder than the now-departing young girl and her aggressive CPR technique: any woman who didn't want to hook up with a stranger sprawled in the middle of a restaurant parking lot.

The paramedics graciously informed me that all my vital signs were fine. I'd live. They would take me to the emergency room if I wanted, though.

"Will you turn on the lights and siren?"

No.

"Then I'll pass."

Besides, I'd settled on a remedy for my embarrassment: a drink. Not the most prudent thing after flirting with a concussion, but I strode bravely into Callender's, grabbed a seat at the bar and ordered, well, a Sprite, and celebrated my health—and the kindness of strangers. I got double takes from a couple of people who recognized me from my horizontal pose earlier, but what the hell.

I was supposed to be sitting here with, as it turned out, a good-looking woman. We were supposed to be getting to know each other.

Maybe there would have been a second date—or rather, a first official date—and then another and another. Perhaps, to the contentment of Janice and Marty, it could have morphed into something serious. In the words of my would-be date, which now echoed in my throbbing head, who knows?

Alas, I never heard from her again. I didn't have her number, so I couldn't call. When I finally got the nerve to tell Janice and Marty the story, they said Marsha simply told them, "It didn't work out." I don't know if her silence was to protect her shame or mine.

DOES YOUR MAMA KNOW ABOUT ME?

WE MET IN THE ICE CREAM section at Carl's Market on Doheny. Beth and her cousin were debating over Häagen-Dazs versus Ben & Jerry's, and I was asked to mediate. I liked Beth because at thirty-two she was well-read and opinionated; because her eclectic music collection included pop, jazz and Tibetan monk choir recordings. She did administrative work in the offices of the Los Angeles County Museum of Art, but regularly volunteered at skid row missions. She had a smart sense of humor.

I was physically attracted to her. She was tall, like a model. In Los Angeles, where practically everyone is on the lookout for someone even semifamous, her dark curly mane and light green eyes often got her mistaken for actress Amy Irving. While Beth was Jewish, race was never an issue for us. She had friends from all backgrounds. We discussed color as it pertains to the world at large, but our conversations didn't hinder our ability to relate to each other simply as people.

This hasn't always been the case. I've found that some white women think proclaiming a preference for brothers makes them more attractive to black men. This works for some black men—those who date only white women, for sure—but to me it suggests someone chasing a stereotype and not a person.

Then again, for those women, I'm not "black" enough anyway; not meaning hue (though undoubtedly for some that too is a factor), but rather my persona— my talk, my attitude, my interests.

I don't know if I ever had a "type," anyway. An illustrated history of the women I've known would resemble the United Nations: lean, statuesque East Africans; sexy Yugoslavians; arty soul sisters from Harlem; curvy Scots; Austrian intellectuals, jet-black Mormons; proper Jamaicans; English Indians; and East L.A. Latinos. They'd be of disparate age and occupation, their commonality being various levels of tolerance for my crazy ass. My only regret is that I never took the time to learn any of their wonderful languages.

Beth's dating guidelines seemed much the same as mine: She went for character as opposed to physicality or ethnicity. An Israeli raised in Manhattan and Los Angeles, Beth had a cosmo outlook that could be attributed only to parentage. She insisted that I would love her parents, and I did.

Beth's father, a bearded ringer for Gregory Peck, was a forward-thinking law professor; her mother, a saucy sculptor and painter who insists Sirhan Sirhan brushed right by her at Los Angeles's Ambassador Hotel on his way to assassinate Robert Kennedy. They seemed liberal-minded and open.

Beth and I had been dating for almost eight months when I visited her parents' home for the meal they pitched the first Friday of every month for friends. While Beth was in the kitchen with her mother putting the finishing touches on the meal, the professor sequestered me in the handsome study of their tastefully appointed West Los Angeles home.

"I don't think there are two people in the world with more in common than blacks and Jews," said the professor while sipping scotch. On one wall, among assorted awards and honors, was a black-and-white photograph of him and Martin Luther King, Jr., with whom he'd marched against the wishes of his father in Montgomery, Alabama.

"I'm not speaking of the obvious," he said, "not the noses, the kinky hair—I guess I'm referring to the other obvious: the oppression, the slavery, the hardships that both people have faced. You better believe we're in the same boat."

He and I spent the time until dinner discussing how we could change the world, while he flipped through the cable channels.

During the meal, I couldn't help savoring the notion of being black. Perhaps it had something to do with the professor's raving about the courage of the blacks who made up the civil rights movement, folks who risked their lives to change history. He went on about the achievements of blacks in the arts, and how whites frequently rewrote the history of modern industry to exclude black inventors. I sat at the long table of artists, local politicians, writers and businessmen, celebrating my blackness.

The next day, over lunch at the old art deco Bullocks Wilshire building, after I told her how much I enjoyed myself at dinner, Beth hesitated for a minute before telling me that we'd be wasting our time if we continued seeing each other. Her statement surprised me. I thought we were doing well.

"We were," Beth said softly, looking into her chicken salad.

"Is there something wrong?" I asked.

She solemnly explained that last night after I left, her mother, who gave me a parting kiss on the lips, told Beth that she and the professor supported the civil rights movement to help ensure that blacks had an equal footing at jobs, education and housing in America but not an entrée to date their daughter.

I was stunned.

I couldn't believe this attitude came from two people who the night before reveled in a broad-minded view regarding all humanity. When I asked Beth how she felt about this, she was silent before saying she enjoyed being with me.

She said I had qualities she looked for in a man: I was inquisitive about life. Didn't talk just to hear my voice. But, she said, "most Jews are destined to marry other Jews," and that at her age she should probably start the interview process. Gee. Not yet thirty, I wasn't thinking of marriage, but I still felt somehow . . . cheated. I was disappointed that a woman of her independent way would let her parents decide whom she should see. Aren't we were supposed to make decisions like this on our own? She'd dated men who weren't Jewish before. What about—what was his name?—*Badri*, the Moroccan chef? Or that Italian stockbroker she'd told me about? How did her parents feel about them? She just shrugged. "They never met my parents."

I wasn't the first man Beth took to her parents' for dinner, but she invited me only because she figured her parents and I would like one another. "They were impressed," she stressed, in their defense. "But my mother said you and I spoke to each other with our eyes a lot at the table—whatever that means—and she asked how I felt about you. I was honest. I told her I could seriously get involved. And that's when she and Father weighed in."

There was nothing left to say. Anything more would have sounded like begging. It wasn't unusual for women I'd dated from different cultures to warn me of the prejudiced views of family or friends. That Beth's folks had portrayed themselves so differently is what I think hurt the most. And Beth's inability to tell her parents to go to hell killed the friendship. "I guess in the end, maybe I'm not as open I like to think I am." She sounded as if she'd disappointed herself.

In the elevator down, I shared with her what her father had said about blacks and Jews being in the same boat. "Oh, he feels we're in same boat, all right," Beth said, after giving it a minute of thought. "Just not in the *same* boat." Obviously.

OFF BY A TABLE

AT THE RESTAURANT, my friend and I had just ordered a sumptuous Italian lunch, when on her way to the ladies room the five-ten, blue-jeaned goddess sauntered past our table. She looked like a model, an actress, or both, but without the attitude. When she walked by again, I looked over at my friend just in time to see him hit in the back of the head by Cupid's arrow.

"She just might be the one," he said, straightening up in his seat.

"You never know," I muttered. I'd skipped breakfast. I could have eaten the knife I used to butter my roll. That risotto with lamb sauce was going to be good.

"That could be something," he continued, as if he were really serious about this. Tall, handsome forty-something and easygoing, he was a success in business as a result of his spooky intuition and willingness to move fast.

But while he routinely made mincemeat of lawyers, my buddy was usually too shy to approach women. However, he had a plan, which he relayed to our young waitress with the charming Italian accent.

"I'd like to buy their lunch," he said, motioning to the back of the room. The waitress discreetly looked back to a table where the two women sat, gave a mischievous grin and leaned in to hear more. You could see her quiet excitement at helping someone make a love connection.

He didn't want his gift of lunch revealed until we were gone. "When I leave, give her this," he said, handing the waitress his business card. Given her instructions, the waitress was gone.

"Wouldn't it be easier if you just walked back there and introduced yourself?" I asked. He refused. "Her girlfriend would dog me as soon as I walked away. This is a Hail Mary, I know, but I have to try it."

I debated my point, and then it occurred to me: This is how it happens. Soul mates meet in the strangest ways. One day I'd sit their fabulous-looking children on my knee and tell them how their parents met. I'd thrown myself in the path of destiny, and I needed to get out of the way.

"This is just crazy enough to work," I'd conceded when our waitress, looking concerned, returned with our meal.

"They're getting ready to leave," she said, sounding anxious. With a mischievous grin, another waiter presented the lunch bill for my buddy's future wife. Suddenly, it seemed like the whole restaurant staff had learned of our operation. The hostess, smirking mischievously, offered to help. The chef poked his head out of his cooking station, curious. He was grinning mischievously.

"Leave?" said the bachelor, handing over his credit card. "You can't let them leave yet. I have to be gone before you tell them anything." I looked at their bill. Eighty-seven dollars. I wondered what they were eating back there. "Give them something else," he said. "Give them dessert." Yes, dessert, nodded the hostess. Then my partner turned to me: "Hurry up and eat, brother."

"Hurry up? Man, get up and go back there and talk to that chick. Hurrying through this meal is a sin."

"Look, this is my wife we're talking about," he said. "Eat up."

I'm famished, and just that quick I was caught up, with my risotto, in a love web. Life is not fair. Meanwhile, my friend mused positive. "Something could happen," he declared, between mouthfuls of grilled chicken. This is how winners do it. They talk up the possibilities.

"Wouldn't it be something if she calls? I'd love to get to know a lady like that."

"You will. If nothing else, she's gonna call out of curiosity," I chimed in sympathetically.

"Man, I'm tired of being alone. I could even do a couple of kids with a woman like that."

"Of course you could. Why not?"

Our waitress was back. "Well, they're having dessert now," she sighed, clearly satisfied with herself. The hostess, standing behind her, shook her head affirmatively. My lunch mate smiled his approval, but in a second his face went forlorn. "I thought they were having dessert," he asked. "Yes, they are," replied the waitress. "They're right there," she said, shooting a glance to two woman chatting at a table.

"Oh, no!"

The waitress, bless her heart, had done everything right—for the wrong table. Just as we all realized this, my man's wife-to-be and her friend, oblivious to it all, sauntered out of the restaurant and into the big city, never to be seen again. She was supposed to be the love of my buddy's life, have a couple of kids. Only no one told her. Least of all my buddy. All around, mischievous grins gave way first to shock, and then to uproarious laughter, my friend's laugh the heartiest. Sadly, that day the Love Gods were off by a table. But the Free Lunch God was right on target.

SUBMISSIVELY YOURS

WE MET AT A CHRISTMAS PARTY in a loft in Los Angeles's downtown art and fashion district. She was in the crowded space that was being used as a dance floor. She wasn't really dancing, just kind of rocking back and forth on long legs to Patti Austin's "Love Me to Death" with Lulu, the party's hostess.

She caught me looking and after her dance put herself in my vicinity. When introduced, she repeated my name with a peculiar seductiveness. She would never utter it again after that night.

Her rather forward way was imposing to a young man five years her junior; so were her credentials. Sexy in a Wall Street kind of way, she ran an apparently successful executive search business from her Pasadena home. Her zeal for passionate discussion softened her austere image. We spent most of the evening getting acquainted.

The following morning, I was pleasantly awakened by a phone call from her. The rasp was deeper than I recalled, and last night she had exhibited a knack for conversation that today gave way to a demeanor somewhat halting and reserved. I noticed it again when we spoke that evening and asked the reason for her tentative behavior.

In a monotone calm she told me she was completely captivated.

"But you don't know me," I said.

"I know that you are the one," she replied confidently. "Whatever else you want me to know, you will tell me."

I listened in titillated curiosity as she described herself as an ambitious, winning woman who tells people what to do all day, and at the end of that day wants someone to be in charge of her. Based on the "quiet and strong" way I'd handled myself at Lulu's set, she decided, just like that, I was someone she wanted to "submit" to. As for her reserved state over the phone, she said immense respect is what I was hearing. "Do I need to say more?"

Nope. I knew exactly what I was hearing. Or at least I thought I knew. I'd read about this kind of woman. An "alternative lifestyle" is what Dr. Ruth might deem it; Rick James was more to the point with "Super Freak." I hung up the phone intrigued, excited . . . and absolutely dumbfounded as to what to do next.

"Get yourself a leather outfit and grow a real mustache," advised my next-door neighbor Ward. It was morning and we were standing in his garden in our overwhelmingly gay West Hollywood enclave (I'd been affectionately dubbed the "token straight and black") when the Federal Express man had me sign for a thin tube package about the length of my arm.

I opened it and pulled out a long thin flexible rod with a slight leather tip at one end and, at the other, a leather handle and dangling gold-plated charm with the inscription TO SIR WITH LOVE.

"Lord have mercy," said Ward. As I headed upstairs I heard him say, "If you're not going to use that thing, let me have it."

"It's a riding crop, sir," she cooed into the receiver. She'd sunk deeper into her role of whatever it was she wanted to be to me.

"And what do I do with it?" I said, trying to sound

authoritatively rhetorical but asking, really *What the hell do I do with this?? Jockeys use these things to inspire racehorses across finish lines.*

"You're going to use it to love me, sir," she answered dreamily.

I've yet to meet a woman who didn't like a little burlap with her silk.

A little consensual hair pulling and spanking never hurt nobody. But this woman wanted more than just the occasional rugged romp; her cravings were on another level.

In the days we communicated over the phone, she became more dependent on my "orders." Ward said that with hard-core "submissives," you had to make lists of stuff for them to do, otherwise they'd be lost. Hell, it was enough trying to run my own life.

In my most masterful voice I'd announce, "Today you're going to run your business." That had been the master's orders for almost a week now, and she was growing weary. "You're going to lose me if you don't take care of me, sir," she'd delicately nudge. I didn't want to lose her before getting to know her, but what did "taking care of her" entail? What happened to the rational woman at the Christmas party? My new sense of power was intoxicating, but I was out of my league and had to face it.

At Atlas Bar and Grill I found her right where I "ordered" her to be, sitting on the very last bar stool. With a trench coat fashionably draped over the shoulders of a gray Chanel business suit that showcased those legs, she was more striking than I remembered.

She kissed my hand. I immediately told her I wasn't the guy for this, and her face went long. I ordered a Guinness and delicately inquired how she got this way. "As if I'm a Martian," she snorted. A glass of wine later, however, she recalled a stone-cold father who didn't hit, but verbally belittled her and her mother.

Without a model for a healthy relationship, "normal" romantic alliances were something to be endured. Tenderness from a man was mostly an annoyance. Like this conversation, even: My concern, she said, was making her uneasy. Anyway, she controlled the things she could—how she dressed, her business, her home. The rest she left to men. Thanks in part to dear ol' dad, her idea of love was being emotionally and physically controlled.

Initially, she pursued the usual bad boy type, before discovering there were men who made a science of controlling women and rewarding them with pain. She lovingly recanted her Greatest Hits, if you will, among them a long-term affair, the highlight of which was being beaten into the fetal position on their bedroom floor.

"I can't be that for you, baby," I said. Still, it felt like I was letting go of something I should be holding on to. After all, how many men knew a woman willing to lay herself at their feet?

We headed to the parking lot in a sentimental silence that she broke. "I should have known better," she said bitterly, her venomous breath creating mist in the chilly night air. "Weak motherfuckers like you make me want to puke. The reason you don't want to be with me is because you can't handle a woman like me. You could never give me what I need." She knew how to entice and welt an ego simultaneously. Courtesy of her father, no doubt. She got me.

"You don't know who you're talking to," I said, taking her by the arm and walking her into a shadowy alley behind the Atlas. Instinctively, she peeled off her coat, that Chanel jacket and white blouse until she was holding on to the brick wall with her back to me wearing only a bra, a skirt and the winter air.

I pulled my belt out of my pants, looked around and fixed myself to do this. If you've always known physical pain as just that, pain, it is difficult to grasp the concept of someone digging it. I was going to attempt to now. I pulled back and put the belt across her back. It didn't feel good. Again. The smack sliced the night.

"Harder," she said.

Swat.

"*Harder* . . . Please . . . pull all the way back."

SWAT!

"Yes, baby . . . yes."

SWAT!!

"Give it to me. . . ."

I'd decided I couldn't hit this woman anymore; a woman's voice confirmed my decision: "I'm calling the police on you two right now!" At the end of the alley were silhouettes of what looked to be an older man and woman. I turned their way and my pants began to fall down.

"Listen," said my accomplice, suddenly becoming quite the conventional thinker, "I run a business . . . I can't be here."

"*You* can't be here?? This crazy shit was what you wanted. . . ."

"You're the one holding the belt."

"You're the one in your bra saying, 'Give it to me, baby. . . .' "

"I'm not going to jail tonight," she said, ignoring me. Without further discussion, we dashed, she making a desperate sprint in her bra, skirt and heels and carrying everything else, me following holding up my pants. Atlas customers who'd seen us earlier tried to make sense of the scene.

Seeking refuge in her Mercedes, we laughed.

"Next time I decide to do something like that, take the belt and beat *me* with it."

"Well, prince of darkness, you ain't." She examined her right shoulder and arm. "You got me there . . . there . . . and ooh, there." Her satisfaction with the marks both fascinated and disturbed me. "Well, I guess this is it," she said, with a detached smile. She wasn't going to get what she wanted here, and she was done. Just like that. "It was nice knowing you."

I gave her a halfhearted peck on the cheek, got out of her car and put my belt through the pant loops as I watched her make a right on Wilshire. Cruisin' for a brusin'. Literally.

I've always held that what two willing adults choose to do between themselves, as long as it doesn't hurt anybody, animals or property, should be their business. Lord knows there are exceptions.

SPIRIT IN RED PUMPS

WELL, I'LL BE DAMNED. If it ain't Steeeve Ivy!"

I looked over my left shoulder and tried not to appear completely clueless. "It's me—Dorsey," he said in a tone that was more of a plea than reminder.

Wow. Dorsey Ferguson. We were classmates in high school auto-body class. We even communicated sporadically after graduation. He was here in Oklahoma City, testing the waters called adult life, and I was "away at school"—if that's what you could call two uneventful years at junior college.

We lost touch. Not really sure why, but I suppose for the same reason we weren't really tight in school: Dorsey was popular with the ladies and that took him places, both practically and figuratively, that an introverted teenager like myself didn't go. At about five foot ten and on the stocky side, he was attractive, but moreover, he had an engaging personality. He was never shy about walking right up to a girl and making his interest known, and this seemed to work for him with the girls—even though he was obviously a player.

However, age can be the great equalizer, and some twenty years later, high school social ratings didn't matter. That Saturday evening, we were simply two guys in Bricktown, a stretch of restaurants and bars in downtown Oklahoma City, open to a little company.

Over drinks, while Dorsey hit on every woman in the bar, we compared notes about two decades of living: I'd lost hair. He'd gained a couple of pounds. I was in Oklahoma City visiting family, having long ago rooted myself in Los Angeles. He had stayed here, gotten married and then divorced. It was a rocky marriage that left him with the skewed view that relationships—serious ones, anyway—were one big bag of tricks. "She made me show her who I really am—made me let her see me cry, and I ain't let nobody see that," he said, motioning to the bartender for another Courvoisier, "and then she stomped all over me. Played on me, fucked up my credit—the whole nine. It's cool, though, because she taught me a lesson: Now, emotionally, I give you nothing. Keep my shit tucked in."

Remarkably, after this dismal testimony, Dorsey conceded that he'd like nothing better than to be in a relationship. Marriage, he said, taught him that he was a "partner person."

Doesn't that involve being everything you just said you didn't want to be with a woman?

"Well, when I find the right woman, my heart will open," he reasoned nonchalantly, as if he could simply call up trust and openness when the time was right. "My mother said you can make that kinda shit happen by 'claiming' it. Now, I don't put a lot of stock in that stuff. That's why I'm out here tonight." He laughed. "Tryin' to 'claim' me somethin'."

Then, as if he'd suddenly been hit with an idea hammer, Dorsey asked me what I was doing tomorrow morning.

"Nothing, really."

"Let's go to church."

"Church?"

It wasn't that he had become especially religious

over the years. Rather, as the line of thinking has forever gone, church was where you found the decent
women, and Dorsey, eternally on the prowl, said he'd
been told by one of his boys about a church on the out-
skirts of the city where the gospel music was good and
the women aplenty.

"I don't know, man. Going to church just to meet
women? Plus, I'll be gone in a couple of days. Why
bother meeting someone . . ."

"Well, you like music, don't you? Come for the
music. C'mon man, I don't wanna check the place out by
myself."

How bad a destination could church be?

I got to Dorsey's place Sunday morning at about
nine. He insisted on driving, which I didn't have a
problem with, and directed my rented Taurus through
the heart of the city's black community and out into
the sticks until we came to a sign on the highway's
right shoulder that read PRAISE CENTER. We pulled onto
a gravel road leading to a large structure in the distance and found a spot in the dusty, red dirt lot, which
was filling up fast. Before getting out of the car,
Dorsey straightened his tie in the rearview mirror and
turned to me. "Hey, man—how you feelin' about
this?"

"I think it works. Isn't that one of those power ties?"

"Not the tie. Us doing this. I mean, you not gon' go up in here and get all sanctified on me, are you?"

"Only if they break into some Marvin. If they play 'Got to Give It Up,' I might embarrass you."

"I'm serious, man. We don't have to be here long. We'll look around for a while and then go get something to eat. All I'm sayin' is, don't lose your cool up in here."

"Boy, you crazy. I gotcha, though. Don't worry."

We made the short pilgrimage from the lot with the rest of God's children—young and middle-aged couples, Bible-toting senior citizens and three-generation families. If there was an overabundance of single women here, they were already inside. Before it became a house of worship, the expansive, box-shaped Praise Center looked as though it might have been a warehouse or an automotive garage. Its current owners had built a reception area of sorts up front, so that you didn't just walk into the place. The low, seductive purr of an organ wafted like a beckoning aroma from the pulpit, where a bass player and drummer were still setting up.

In our survey of the congregation we could see, among the others, adult women of all ages, several of them quite attractive. A few were sitting with a girlfriend or a family member. In other words, single. It wasn't exactly the Land of Ladies Dorsey's boy played it up to be, but the numbers met the approval of Dorsey, now confident that our expedition would not be a bust. 'This what I'm talkin' 'bout!" he declared glowingly, seeking to convince himself of the possibilities. He turned to a table holding pamphlets, bulletins and paper fans, picked up a clipboard and began to write.

"What are you doing?"

"I'm putting our names on the visitor's list."

"Dorsey, we don't need to do all that. They'll be calling our names and we'll have to stand up. . . ."

"That's the whole idea. Everyone will know we in the house and then we ain't gotta work. We in like flint."

Dorsey's conniving stopped cold when he saw the vision standing in the doorway of the main room. Wearing a black, formfitting skirt, she looked to be in her mid-twenties, her angelic, caramel-colored face and Bambi nose framed by dark brown Jheri-curled hair.

She was small-breasted, with a narrow waist and thick in the hips and legs; Lord knows it was all there. She was a striking, if somewhat tacky, melange of small-town innocence and rural sexuality perched on red high heels. My first impression was that she was outfitted awfully sexy for Sunday worship, especially when you considered those sheer black Betty Page stockings with sinister seams running down the backs of her spectacularly sculpted legs.

Her white gloves, which cradled a small stack of

church programs, indicated her usher's status. She smiled and shyly introduced herself as Dee Dee, even though her name tag said DAPHINE, and asked us to follow her.

"Oh my goodness," Dorsey whispered as Dee Dee's swaying hips lured us up the aisle.

"That's a fashion faux pas," I said of the young lady's choice of red shoes.

"No, that's called a brick house," Dorsey retorted. "You been in California too long, Ivy."

I mentioned to our sexy usher that we didn't want to sit too far up—seats near the rear would better accommodate a hasty exit. She ignored me, putting us in two folding chairs about ten rows from the front.

Dorsey didn't seem to mind. He would have followed those hips past the choir, through the pulpit, out the back door and into the woods. He sat to my left, just off the aisle; to my right was a lean, mild-mannered elderly woman with a cane, and next to her, a woman she kindly introduced as her sister.

I asked the gentleman sitting in front of us where I might find the men's room. He instructed me to go through the side door, make a right and open the first door I came to. I found the rest room—and a parishioner inside, putting away a flask. I suppose a preservice cocktail never hurt no one.

I returned to my seat in time to hear a voice over the P.A. system command, "Let us rise and praise the Lord Almighty!" On cue, the rhythm section jumped into a dynamic, hearty groove, and the congregation responded by jubilantly singing along—swaying, clapping their hands and slapping tambourines.

At most of the churches I've visited, the energy level usually builds over the course of the service. At the Praise Center, it was like an R&B concert; the emotionally charged audience was into it from the very beginning.

After that first song, which lasted about two days, they handled church business: details of a fund-raising picnic; prayers for the "sick and shut-in" and, the part I dreaded, the introduction of church visitors. We weren't the only ones, but when a deacon gave particular attention to my visiting from "Los AngeLEES, CalaPHONia," folks strained to get a look at the two new sinners in the house. "See that lil' honey checking you out over there?" Dorsey encouraged as we sat down. "You exclusive, nigga—they want us."

The Praise Center's reverend—a thin, nattily dressed middle-aged man with the mandatory gold tooth and a guttural squall that blues singer Bobby "Blue" Bland would have killed for—was the kind of Bible thumper who felt he hadn't done his job if the building was still standing after his sermon. Like the best theatrical pastors, he started softly, taking his time and setting up the emotions of his flock before closing in for the kill. Or perhaps this was simply the effect alcohol had on his performance, as this was the cat with the flask I'd seen in the men's room.

It was at the Praise Center that I officially grasped the conspiratorial relationship between preacher and church organist. To be sure, they are in cahoots. The Word incites, but it is the melodious, holy vibration of a Hammond B-3 rattling your lower intestines that pushes you over the edge. An enlightened organist will stalk a preacher's every word, supplying a sermon its heart-tugging musical drama. In no time, they had driven this congregation to the Promised Land.

That previously indispensable cane belonging to the little old lady to my right was now lying on the floor, as she sprang up in a fit of trancelike joy, backhanding me in the process. The odd man or woman, overcome by the Spirit, pranced up and down the aisles like proud roosters and hens. These folk had come to lay their burdens down and were getting their tithings' worth.

Shouting wasn't anything new to me. I recall Sundays as a child at Faith Memorial Baptist. After church, Mama and my sister, Barbara, would kick off their shoes, plop down on the living room couch and review the service like two theater critics, cackling about what shouters had found Reverend Curry's thunderous performance irresistible.

However, the pandemonium at the Praise Center was on a level that I found unsettling. I hadn't witnessed the release of this many endorphins under one roof since the bill of Parliament/Funkadelic and Bootsy's Rubber Band sold out the Los Angeles Forum in 1977. It was only a matter of time before someone lost a wig or a set of dentures. The preacher, smelling blood, bit into his sermon's climax with the might of a pit bull and wouldn't let go: ". . . AND GODAH SAID . . . I SAID, AND GODAH SAID, I'MMMMMMM NOT GOIN' BACK!! I'MMMMMMM NOT GOIN' BACK!! . . ."

When the choir began to sing again, I decided I'd seen enough. I nudged Dorsey, but got no response and turned to discover tears streaming down his cheeks. Just a few minutes ago he was snickering at the random "well"s and "all right now"s being offered up by the congregation. I wondered at what point had Reverend Gold Tooth gotten to him, how long he'd been standing here silently filled with the Holy Ghost.

"You all right, brother?" I asked. He slowly nodded his head affirmatively. I suggested we go get something to eat, but he just stood there.

At that moment, my eyes met with those of an older

female deacon in the pulpit. She quickly discerned my emotional state, and then scrutinized Dorsey with the concentrated gaze of a tiger set to pounce on its prey before promptly setting two chairs in front of the congregation. I knew what that meant: Those chairs were for new meat plucked from the handful of visitors.

"Dorsey, we need to go," I said, eyeing the deacon, now making her way down the aisle. "They comin' to get you, man."

Dorsey didn't respond.

Too late.

"What is your name, dear?" she asked with the aplomb of a school marm.

"Dorsey," he uttered through his tears.

"Praise the Lawd. Come wit' me, brother Dorsey." She laced her white-gloved hands on his shoulder and forearm, as if to comfort him, but her hold also made it easy to direct the dazed and confused up the aisle. He looked over at me as if to ask, "How did this happen?"

"Don't look to your friend, baby, look to Christ. Come to God, brother Dorsey. You comin' too," she said sternly, cutting her eyes at me.

"Uh, I'm from Los Angeles . . ."

"And? He the king uh kings, young man—He run it all— CalaPHONia, too."

"Yes, ma'am, I know God is in Los Angeles. I

just . . ." This was not the time nor the place to debate religion versus spirituality—or Gold Tooth's penchant for getting his drink on before addressing his congregation.

"Come, brother Dorsey."

"Dorsey, man, you sure you wanna do this?"

" 'Course he's sure—this why he came here." I had to chuckle to myself. If she only knew why Dorsey had come here. The choir continued to wail. Folks whooped, hollered and stomped as the deacon and I engaged in a tug-of-war for Dorsey's soul. For a minute, he was snapping out of it—at which point the tough deacon pulled out all the stops and motioned toward the pulpit for reinforcements.

Down the aisle came the mighty hips of one Dee Dee. She took one look at Dorsey, smiled and extended her white-gloved hand. His grip on my arm loosened. The battle was over.

They led him up the aisle slowly—the sexy usher's arm around his waist—and put their conquest on display in one of the chairs. The congregation roared as Dorsey sat before them, weeping like a baby. Player was no match for the Holy Ghost and big legs in red pumps.

After the service, I went up and gave Dorsey a hug. His face, puffy from a river of salty tears, resembled that of a boxer who'd won the round but lost the fight. As the sexy usher consoled him, another church member wrote down the new member's information. They told me to leave him. Said Brother somebody or another would see that Dorsey got home.

I got a message from Dorsey recently. He and Dee Dee—I mean, Daphine—have been married for several years now and have two sons. The family, he said into my answering machine, was relocating to Europe, being sent there by the car manufacturer he worked for.

I never had the opportunity to discuss it with him, but in retrospect, I suspect it happened just as Dorsey's mother said it would. The process no doubt began that Saturday night in Bricktown, when Dorsey and I were drinking and he unwittingly made a declaration of love. I'll be doggone if Dorsey, a man who said he didn't believe in "all that old mess," didn't walk into the Praise Center and find himself a wife. *Willed* her, just like that.

REAL MEN BUY THEM IN SUPERMARKETS

ONE EVENING A FEW YEARS BACK, while grocery shopping at the supermarket, I took a deep breath and spontaneously pushed the envelope: I decided to buy a box of condoms.

I should not have a problem buying condoms, and I don't. To my mind, that's what all-night pharmacies are really for anyway. At about 10 P.M. after most of the customers are in bed vegging out on their prescriptions, I covertly make my purchase, forgoing the front counter and paying the pharmacist directly.

However, buying condoms in a supermarket is a different kind of party.

Seeking out Trojan Man in broad fluorescent light while facing all that humanity (read: women and children) somehow seems just short of trench coat–clad perversion

My self-consciousness is undoubtedly some stale residue from the sexually repressed early sixties of my youth, when sex was what you did to make a family, married TV couples slept in twin beds and *Playboy* magazine was considered indecent. Of course, on the downlow, there was plenty gettin' down going on. And condoms, worn as a safeguard against sexually transmitted diseases, were basically the only form of birth control.

The sexual revolution of the late sixties and the pill changed how society approached sex, but it didn't change the condom. It still pretty much came in one size and would often break during sex—that is, if there *was* sex.

Most times, my partner would lie beside me in frustration as I'd fumble in horrific futility, trying to get the damn thing on, my manhood literally and figuratively shrinking.

The condom took on crucial new significance in 1983 when American Dr. Robert Gallo and French Dr. Luc

Montagnier announced their chilling discovery of HIV. Until a cure is found, abstinence aside, the first line of defense against the deadly mother of all STDs, researchers advised was . . . the archaic, unreliable condom? Previously complacent condom manufacturers, now competing for a vast global market, began listening to the consumer. They made condoms with more durability, in more sizes and even in glow-in-the-dark colors.

Because they were so vital, suddenly condoms were in.

They were the responsible thing to do—which was why I told myself I shouldn't be worried about how I'd look buying condoms to grocery shoppers.

So why, as I stood in aisle 5 perusing the selection, did I feel as if I resembled an eager horndog? A woman with her young son was heading down the aisle toward the Slimfast. When she noticed where I was standing, she slowed her pace. It was now or never. I pulled the black box with distinctive gold lettering from the display, threw it into my shopping cart and headed for the checkout lines.

Ah, what luck: A male cashier had just opened his lane. I slid through, gratified until a man and his teenage daughter pulled up immediately behind me. All this self-consciousness is ridiculous, I told myself, and quickly unloaded my basket.

The conveyor belt began to move. Bread . . . ice

cream . . . fruit . . . mayonnaise . . . bottled water . . . BIG
BLACK BOX OF CONDOMS . . . cookies. . . . Everything
was going well. Then the items abruptly ceased moving.
Weighed down by that BIG BLACK BOX OF CON-
DOMS. An entire line of anxious customers leaned for-
ward to see what the difficulty was.

The father smirked at the box. His daughter nervously turned away. The father gave me a disdainful
glare—as if I were just the kind of condom-packin',
daughter-stalking scum for whom he kept a loaded shot-
gun by his bed.

The cashier nonchalantly dragged that BIG BLACK
BOX across the scanner. Nothing. Again. Nothing. The
collective, weary sigh of customers. Again. Nothing. It
was about then that everything appeared to move in
slow motion: The cashier reached for his microphone for
a price check, but then turned to my terrified eyes that
begged, "Don't do this . . . please." I wanted to explain
to the line—hell, just take the microphone and announce to the whole damned supermarket—"Look, I'm
not doing anything wrong here. I'm not a criminal or a
whore. I simply bought condoms in a supermarket to
prove to myself I could do so without shame."

The cashier looked at my anguished face and had
mercy.

He pushed the BIG BLACK BOX aside and rang up

the rest of my things. He bagged my groceries—and then quickly tossed in the BIG BLACK BOX with an expression that said, "It's on me, bro."

Life is about facing fears, no matter how big, small or completely asinine. My torment over paying for condoms along with milk and eggs was silly, but I stared down the situation and it blinked. I'll admit, I've since returned to the shadows of adult bookstores and midnight pharmacies for my condom purchases. I'm not trying to be nobody's martyr—they gotta get the kinks out of those conveyor belts.

Besides, after my dating sabbatical, finding someone compatible proved a more formidable task. However, had anything come up, I'd have been prepared. I had an open heart and a BIG BLACK BOX OF CONDOMS that I paid for with my last nerve.

I'LL TAKE MANHATTAN— THE REST IS HERS

I SALIVATED AS I SUGGESTED lunch at the Broadway Deli in Santa Monica. I hadn't been there in months, but was willing to brave crowds drawn to the Pacific Ocean on a Saturday afternoon to satisfy a pregnant woman's kind of hankering I had for their turkey chili—with a vanilla malt.

I figured my notion of gastronomic delight was what made him go silent, but after several seconds more, he finally spoke up. "Man, I can't do the Deli," he said with resignation. "Especially on a weekend. That's her place."

"Huh?"

"It's hers," he said again, as if annoyed I hadn't immediately gotten it the first time, and a little embarrassed to repeat it. "It's her spot; I have to respect that."

It had been about six months since they split after five years of living together, and he'd been doing so well that I'd forgotten his pain. As for the other part—the idea that, for him, the Broadway Deli was one of the things that went when *she* went—that, I understood perfectly.

In the state of California and possibly others, unless detailed provisions have been made in happier times, when a couple divorce, property is generally split evenly. "Half!" is the disdainful cry of whoever has the most to lose.

However, that decree simply covers material things. Whether you are divorcing, separating or simply coming off a long-term relationship, also at stake are ethereal accoutrements governed by an unspoken law. Thus, hangouts, friends, even family members, all become pawns in the ritual of getting on with one's life.

Everything on earth abides by a rule, absurdities included, and the axiom determining who gets a favorite bar or taco stand in the event of a breakup is simple: Whoever turned the other on to the place keeps it.

My friend's girlfriend was the first person to take

him to the Broadway Deli, and it's not as if she simply *likes* the place. Before they met, she'd spent serious chunks of her life there, studying for the bar in a booth by the window that stretches along Broadway; at the counter, watching her waiter-neglected hot roast beef sandwich cool on the service deck; on the outdoor patio sipping mimosas and watching humanity stroll the promenade. That's her place, and not even a glib-tongued Johnnie Cochran can alter this.

Location Division after a breakup is the reason pop songs whine, ". . . All the places we *used* to go." The next verse never explains that one of them is still going to that place, but the message, to one of the two, is clear, nonetheless: Stay out of Gannelli's Italian Buffet. It's mine. I was going there long before I knew you existed, before I even liked boys. You got the DVD player, and you ruined my favorite comforter, so take it. But eat your lasagna elsewhere. You never knew good Italian before you met me anyway, so you should be fine anywhere.

Sentimental haunts are not all that are divvied up after a split. I know a guy who inherited an uncle. His wife put up with her own mother's brother only because the uncle and her husband got along so well. When they divorced, her ex and Uncle Art both sighed "good riddance."

Individual Favorite Songs—the ditty you dug simply because she dug it—those revert to the individual. "Our

Song"—the tune you discovered together and adopted as the theme of your undying love—well, that tune is just ass out of luck, an orphan, like so many dog-eared photos of a once happy couple, discarded by both parties perhaps for all time, or at least until it doesn't pain you to hear it.

It's not like this for everyone. There are couples who, after the storm clears, can not only be cordial but socialize with each other. With their exes' new mates, even. The latter might be a stretch for most, but truth be told, if, after the requisite bitterness, you and the person with whom you shared a bed and a toilet seat can't enjoy the occasional double king cheese at her favorite burger stand or a cosmopolitan at his favorite bar, then you were both fooling yourselves about what you had in the first place. It happens.

I told my buddy that it is a big world out there and he owed it to himself to discover more of it. We could begin with downtown L.A., at a little hole-in-the-wall with two distinctions. One, the grilled fish sandwich will make you do the Snoopy dance. Two, none of the customers told their partners about this joint in the first place.

RULES TO BE BROKEN

THE BULLSHIT BEGINS with hello: You chat awhile and then give her your number because you don't want to invade her privacy by asking for hers. Then again, perhaps you *should* ask for her number, lest she be one of those women who doesn't call men.

I was educated on this bit of lunacy by just such a woman. We'd gone out a couple of times and, from all indications, enjoyed ourselves. However, I noticed that while she welcomed my calls, not once did I pick up my receiver and find her voice on the other end. When I casually inquired about this, she responded with nonchalance, "Oh, I don't call men."

Perplexed, I asked her to expound, and she said it simply never occurred to her to call a man; that was his job.

She obviously relished hearing from men who thought enough to reach out; didn't she think he'd appreciate the same gesture?

"I'm sure he probably would," she acknowledged.

"Then why don't you—"

"I don't call men," she said again, irritated with my lack of comprehension. We bandied over this a while longer before shifting the conversation to something innocuous enough to get us off the phone with a modicum of civility. I wouldn't call again, and since she didn't call men, I didn't have to worry about hearing from her. Of course, I have long since learned that in the universe of relationships, there are rules. For instance, if a man does get a woman's phone number, he doesn't dare use it for a minimum of, say, two days. Minimum. Three days is ideal. Otherwise, even though deep down both might want to communicate much sooner, she is going to see him as desperate, and he will be concerned that it looks as if he has nothing—or anyone—else to do.

The first time she returns your call, you should not

pick up even if you're available. This way, you will get to hear the answering-machine message, and that is where the real information lies. People often express more to a machine than to a breathing person, even if the revelations are found only in the speaking tone. She might leave only her name, number and the best time to return her call, but whether she says so sweetly or perfunctorily can indicate her interest level. But then, this is only if they leave a message at all.

Fellas, when you take her out, pick up the tab. I know—you wouldn't have it any other way. Maybe it would be impressive if she feigned a reach for the cocktail bill or dinner check—at least then you'd feel like you were more than just her meal ticket that night. But keep the idea of her showing that kind of consideration to yourself, or risk being seen as one cheap son of a bitch.

I could go on, but I won't; it's too depressing. Suffice it to say that in my exhaustive examination of the rules—of living by some and breaking others—I have learned two important things. One, that while there are rules and then there are *rules,* every one of them, large and small, holds significance.

The rules most likely germinated in the Garden, where Eve persuaded Adam, the First Man to Get Played (first famous last words: "Come to think of it, all that day she'd been actin' kinda funny. . . .") to partake in the forbidden fruit. The Bible, however, doesn't mention what certain historians now speculate—that additionally, the snake slipped Eve a mimeographed three-page double-spaced document, believed to be the rules. Number two, I've learned that ultimately these rules, the whole nasty lot, are steeped in the foul art of not sharing one's true emotions. Think about it: The mother of all rules is one that says, at least in the beginning, it is wrong to reveal to a potential partner how you really feel. Men and women have nurtured the rules as a way of concealing unwarranted insecurities and fear of rejection.

It's all bullshit, and everyone who plays by the rules knows it's bullshit, but these are the rules, and they've been the rules for so long, almost everyone participates. If you don't, you, an otherwise emotionally healthy human being, risk not getting to know a person who likewise appears to be perfectly sane but for his or her willingness to conceal true feelings in hopes of finding a . . . fulfilling relationship built on communication, respect and trust. Disregard the rules and he or she is going to think you desperate, lonely, needy, weak or just plain weird.

But you know what? As of this writing, I'm done with the rules. I mean it. Fuck the rules. The next time I meet someone who interests me, I am going to give her my number. If she reciprocates, I might even phone her on my way home just to say that I had a great time meeting her. If she calls me as I'm coming in the door, I am going to run to the phone and pick it up mid-message and tell her that I was hoping she'd call. In the coming days I will let her know that I am attracted to her personality and unusual but kind-of-sexy swagger, that I'd like to know more and that making this apparent doesn't mean I am needy or any of the other things that might inspire her to unleash a crucifix and some garlic to ward me off. When she reaches for the tab, I will be even happier to pay it.

I'm going to take a dip in the Pacific Ocean, even though I know the water isn't what it used to be; I want to sneak into a movie I didn't pay to see. I want to live dangerously. And break all the rules.

PART II

FOR BETTER OR WORSE: THE BLUEPRINT

THE FIRST WOMAN IN MY LIFE

THE LAST TIME I SAW Marjorie Ivory she was sitting on the couch in our living room, holding a glass of something. In one of those one-piece button-down housedresses she often wore, slippers parked next to her bare feet, she was wearing that blissful gaze Mama would have when she was pleased.

When Mama was happy, her children were happy. That Friday evening, November 28, 1971, was no exception. Earlier, she and Bryn Bacey, a family friend, had gone Christmas shopping. Though she didn't reveal much from the bags—after all, they were Christmas gifts, to be wrapped and put under the tree—she seemed satisfied with the spoils.

Barbara, my twenty-one-year-old sister, already the mother of toddler John Eric and due to give birth again any day, was home waiting on her husband, Ronnie, also living with us, to return from an errand. My younger brothers, thirteen-year-old Tony and eight-year-old Kevin, lounged around the living room.

The television in the living room was on, but no one was really watching. Its volume was way down low, as cool sounds from the FM stereo permeated our three-bedroom abode like a soothing, sonic incense. The house felt so warm and cozy and of good spirit that I almost didn't want to step out into the winter chill to go watch my Douglass High School Trojans play basketball.

But eating at me that night was an unusually strong urge to get out of the house, and classmate Keith Hammons, in his Impala, was out front honking anxiously.

Just before I walked out the door, Mama gave me a look I will never forget. She cast upon me an expression of motherly love and affection that I hadn't seen in a long time, no doubt held hostage by the daily grind of making a living and raising her family alone. "Have a good time," she said simply, with a slight, warm smile.

"I will," I replied, attempting to conceal my shyness at her show of love by looking down and fumbling with the buttons on the dark blue full-length wool coat that in '71 was my pride and joy. (When the Jackson 5 came to town and Don Minnis and I crashed their noon rehearsal at the Myriad Convention Center, I caught Jermaine, himself sporting a cool full-length number with fake fur, discreetly checking out my coat. It was a bad coat.)

That fleeting moment between Mama and me might have been the beginning of a new level of communication between a parent and a child not yet mature enough to see his mother as a full-fledged person. As it was, in my eyes, the role of parents was simply to provide food, shelter and school lunch money.

I did have a good time at the game, though. I hated school but loved attending the sporting events. Once there, I let my buddy Hammons do the strolling and profiling that kids did at these things. I just sat there, cheering the Trojans while fantasizing about the teen life I privately longed for.

I imagined being the star player on the team and hitting that jump shot; imagined playing that funky drum cadence in the school band that sat in the rafters supplying the music. I figured either occupation would get me the attention of one of those big-legged cheerleaders down on the floor.

Sufficiently high from witnessing another Trojans victory, I declined Hammons's invitation to check out a house party and had him drop me off at home. Must have been about ten o'clock. Before I could get my key in the front door, my brother-in-law opened it.

"Say you're not going to freak out when I tell you what happened," pleaded Ronnie. I'd never seen him like this. He looked really nervous. My first thought was that he and Barbara, who had a propensity for getting physical during their disagreements, had had yet another argument. I liked Ronnie, but as a brother devoted to his sister, I'd confronted him before when he and Barbara got into it. I wasn't a fighter, but was willing to go there nonetheless. Thank God Mama had stood between us at the time.

But as Ronnie spoke, I noticed Kevin in a chair and Tony on the couch, their faces swollen from tears. Both seemed so preoccupied with their thoughts that they never even looked up at me. "Margie got sick," Ronnie said. "Barbara went with her in the ambulance." I didn't know what to think, although it all looked very serious. Before I could gather my thoughts, Ronnie was instructing Tony to stay with Kevin and the baby. He and I hopped into his green '65 Mustang to go to University Hospital.

En route he explained that Mama had been complaining of a headache and went to her bedroom to lie down. In a minute, though, she called out to Barbara. "I think I'm having a stroke," she was able to mutter, before losing consciousness.

Barbara called for an ambulance while Tony and Kevin looked on in horror. She sought to revive Mama, attempting to pry open her mouth with a spoon so she could perform CPR, but she couldn't get her mouth open.

When we got to the hospital, Barbara was sitting in a hallway outside the emergency room, trying to keep it together. The whole hospital floor was in organized chaos, with nurses and doctors busy handling all kinds of emergencies. A nurse told us it would be a while and to be patient. I stuck around for about twenty minutes before walking down the hallway and out an exit door into the still, cold night. I needed to get a grip. And have a private talk with the Man upstairs.

We weren't a super religious family, but I believed. I'd had many a talk with God in my young life, about any number of trivialities—like earlier that week promising Him I'd study if He saw me through a desperate moment at the blackboard in math class. But this was an SOS on another level and required a special commitment.

"God, I'll be the perfect human being from here on out,

if you just don't take our Mama," I begged, tears streaming down my cheeks. I'd broken promises to Him before, but I really meant it this time. And while this would be a close one, I knew that in the end, God would come through.

By the time I got back to the hallway where I'd left Barbara and Ronnie, a couple of family friends had gathered. It was after midnight now, and still no word on Mama's condition. Sitting on the floor next to a chair, I blocked out the voices around me with prayers in my head. I fell asleep, only to be awakened maybe twenty minutes later by my sister's bloodcurdling wail. Standing over me was a doctor, a nondescript white man in a white hospital coat, and he had a pained look on his face. Just like in a TV drama, he was solemnly telling us that he was sorry, nothing more could be done. I didn't cry. I suppose I was in shock. I'd attempted to bribe God, but He had other plans all along.

I remembered how as a child I could bring myself to tears simply imagining Mama's passing. But this was real. Just that quick, Marjorie Ivory, my mother and the first woman in my life, was gone. I was fifteen years old.

Most children come to know their parents as they themselves become adults. Not having that privilege, I had to piece together a puzzle consisting of my memories and other people's and make a few deductions to get a complete picture.

The first thing I had to face about her was that she wasn't perfect. Of course, I knew this much while she lived. However, knowing it doesn't matter when a loved one passes. Almost immediately they are exalted by family and friends to sainthood. It took me years to see that Mama was just a person, with hopes, dreams and faults. For example, with a schoolgirl's zeal, she dreamed of one day getting a master's degree in child development; the reality was that not everything that went wrong in their marriage was all Daddy's fault, and like all of us in this life, her simple hope was that at the end of the day, everything would be all right.

Her name wasn't even always Ivory. Once upon a time it was Turner, the last name of her father, Gather Turner, a tall, handsome man who didn't say much and couldn't hold his liquor. He gave his wife, Jessie, three girls, the oldest of whom would become my mother.

Like her father, Mama was largely elusive in her physical expression of love. Clearly, she loved her children, was proud of us and always encouraged us to do well. But after we reached a certain age, the fawning ceased.

Perhaps because of this, it was natural for me to spend an inordinate amount of time alone. To be sure, being comfortable with my own company served me well in growing up without a mother.

Still, I would have loved Mama's opinion and/or wisdom on the many facets of this life. I never got to turn to her or pick up a phone, present her with a situation and ask her what I should do. I wonder what she would have to say about her middle child becoming a writer? As two adults, would we have even gotten along? Indeed, my biggest regret is that she never knew me as a man.

Nevertheless, innately, from Mama I learned many things. Especially about women. For instance, I know that even in a bad relationship, good sex can go a long way. I remember how pleasant Mama would be in the days after Daddy took me out of their bed during the night, put me in bed with my brothers and closed the door. I don't know exactly what went on in there, but for the next several days after Daddy made his midnight move, Mama would be particularly mellow.

And I know when a woman is fed up. She doesn't have to say a word. Her body language will speak volumes of her discontent. When she slowly stops doing the little things for her man— preparing his plate for him during meals; running his bathwater—and is short with him during their every communication, she is sending a signal.

Mama worked as a teacher in the government's inner-city Headstart program of the '60s and '70s. While she found the job rewarding, a roomful of energetic preschoolers often danced on her last nerve. Then she'd come home and cook and clean and negotiate the problems of her own brood.

To associates, she appeared to be a superwoman. Only immediate family and close friends knew that, without fail, at the end of every grueling week Mama sought in a bottle of gin comfort from the pain of her life. You never know what cross even the most seemingly "together" woman bears, or what she is liable to embrace to console herself. I learned this by watching Mama.

Meeting a new man after years of loneliness and celibacy can do wonders for a single parent's disposition. I know this because as a child I saw Mama's outlook change dramatically when she began to date in the months before her death.

Thanks to Mama, I know that at the core of most women, no matter their culture or background, is a fragile, hopeful little girl. I've seen some very successful, powerful women at the end of a business day revert to tender, vulnerable souls with childlike voices.

I didn't know I was learning these things when I learned them; during my short relationship with Mama, they seeped into my subconscious.

But because of what I took from my precious time

with her, I believe Mama would have liked the women with whom I've had my most serious relationships. She would be attracted to their dedication, domestic ingenuity, inquisitive natures and forward thinking.

Mama might have even reprimanded me about botching a couple of those relationships in particular; in them she might have seen a woman good for her son. But she would have liked these women. Because in each of them, she would have found a little of herself.

ACT OF LOVE
#1,345

IT WAS THE LATE EIGHTIES. After a three-year live-in relationship had come to an end, I was, as the song says, alone again naturally—a fact underscored that first week by changing the linens on my bed without the help of a partner.

The sight of a fresh, floating top sheet reminded me of those occasions as a child when my mother made the bed—with me in it.

Just why this would happen varied. Sometimes Mama was adding a blanket in preparation for a particularly chilly Oklahoma night. Or I could have been ill with a cold or the dreaded tonsillitis, which would usually leave me bedridden a couple of times a year. Most times, though I'd simply call myself "helping" Mama change the sheets, but wouldn't properly tuck them in at the corners. After getting frustrated with having to come behind me and redo the job, she'd tell me to just get in the bed and let her get it done.

In any case, there I'd be, sprawled on the bare mattress in flannel pajamas imprinted with little cowboys and Indians or spaceships or some other image that characterized boy's pajamas, as Mama went about the deed.

It was a process that actually began, of course, with washing the bedding. Sometimes we'd walk the couple of blocks to the laundromat on Eighth Street, but quite often Mama would wash our clothes at home. This was the mid-sixties and, at least in our neighborhood, not every home was equipped with a washer, not even the manual kind.

Armed with a washboard and good old-fashioned elbow grease, Mama would sit on the side of a bathtub filled with warm water and Oxydol detergent and get busy. After thoroughly washing, rinsing and wringing out a tubful of clothes and bedding, she'd load up that deep, durable wicker basket, grab the bag of clothespins, head out into the backyard and hang our clothes out on the line to be tended to by nature's dryer—warm sunshine and fresh air.

That evening, when making my bed, she'd start with the fitted bottom sheet, instructing me to get on it after she'd secured the first two corners. She'd then fit the other corners, stuffing the pillowcases after that.

In all her life, I don't ever remember Mama saying to me, "I love you." But I'd look at her face as she dutifully made her way around the bed—her lips pursed as they were when she concentrated on something—and witness the divine contentment of a mother caring for her child. Her apparent reward was my quiet elation that, despite her having three other sons and a daughter, at least for a moment I had my mother's undivided attention.

For me, the best part of the bed changing came when, finally, Mama would unfold the top sheet. She'd vigorously unfurl it over me and the bed, and I'd squeal in delight at the blissful, surreal sensation of that sheet floating above me at first, then descending seemingly in slow motion, like a detergent-scented cloud, onto the bed and my body. It felt dreamy—like love coming in for a landing. Seemingly for my thrill's sake, Mama would repeat the spread. And then she'd do the same thing with the blanket. What a way to hit the hay, at the loving hands of a parent.

Many momentous occasions happen on one's way to adulthood: a child's first steps, college graduation, marriage, divorce. But there are also many little things that shape a big life: permission to go to a movie theater alone; a father's knowing glance; the amazing discovery that once, your parents were young—any number of nonevents that don't appear to mean much until you're on your own. Then it occurs to you that somebody once took care of you, committed themselves indiscriminately to the big and little things. And they did so out of love.

Marjorie Ivory did things far more important for me than make my bed. When you look back as a grown-up, you realize that there are no little things—only a parent's acts of love. I often think about that when I am alone, changing my own sheets.

MAMA HAD
A KUNG FU GRIP

IN THE SUPERMARKET, a mother was having a dispute with her son, who looked to be about nine years old.

"I said that's it, I don't want to discuss it again, ever! And don't bring it up again!"

This was the kid talking.

He stormed out of the cereal aisle, followed by his mother, who—looking equal parts frustrated and embarrassed—told him he had a "time out" coming when they got home.

Little Johnny's tirade brought to mind the ongoing debate I have with friends regarding parental discipline. I happen to be one of those archaic souls who think that, just sometimes, physical discipline is in order.

I don't have kids, but I used to be one, and I learned early in life that there was a price to be paid for my actions, and sometimes it wasn't simply verbal.

Had that been my mother, "time" would have stopped right there on aisle 5. With rows of cornflakes, Cocoa Puffs, the Trix rabbit and Cap'n Crunch all bearing witness, a child would have had a revelation. To be honest, I can count the spankings I got at home. My four siblings and I were never what you'd call cutups.

Marjorie Ivory was a gentle woman, not the kind of ear-tugging, verbally abusive parent who gives discipline a bad name. Usually, she'd simply give you a certain gaze, and time would stop. When all else failed—and there wasn't much "else" beyond a second or third "I thought I told you not to do that"—she sent me out into the backyard to pluck the tool of my punishment. In my childhood ingenuity, I never realized that it was the skinniest, puniest branch that stung little brown legs the most.

If, on the rare occasion I did "show out" in public, naked eyes simply saw a loving mother calmly taking her child by the arm; onlookers didn't know Mama had a kung fu grip.

This kind of lovin' extended to school. Were there any teachers in my elementary and junior high schools not packing heat—a rubber hose or a souped-up wooden paddle—in their desk drawers?

Certainly there was the odd parent in the principal's office, raising hell about the teacher who "laid hands on my child." But right or wrong, physical reprimand was as much a part of school life as fish sticks on Friday.

Under the weight of such a looming threat, class-room conspiracies caved in swiftly and mercilessly; if the culprit didn't come forward or wasn't offered up to the teacher by his classmates, the classroom door would be closed, the whole class would be lined up and everyone would pay for the jive of a few. The lesson: While authority is away, you will govern yourselves and order will prevail.

Carter Woodson Elementary's Miss Townsend was the mother of all disciplinarians, a tall, lean proud black woman who ran her classroom the way Khrushchev ran the Soviet Union. You'd peek into her room and see the biggest bully sitting with a halo over his head.

She'd get your attention with words or with a text-book flying in your direction. Today, a teacher could be locked up for such antics. I'd say it was Miss Townsend who ultimately kept a few hardheads out of jail.

Of course, there is another side to all this. There are

youngsters whose problems are not remedied by the proverbial spanking, children who need and deserve the loving care and attention of professional help. And there are those parents and teachers who, under the guise of discipline, methodically abuse children. They too, need professional help—and maybe some jail time.

I'm talking something else here, about putting a train back on its track. About presenting consequences to create a sense of responsibility.

At first I considered Little Johnny lucky that he didn't have to deal with the likes of Marjorie Ivory—and then immediately felt sorry that he doesn't know that kind of attention. Because every now and then we all need someone to put us back on track. Someone who loves us enough to do so.

BIG PURPLE BOX

THIS TIME, Don Minnis downright refused to go to Safeway for his mother. On a blistering Oklahoma city summer day like this one, teenage hoodlum Busta and his gang were sure to be hanging out in the grocery store's parking lot. Donny and I had dodged them enough times.

It took a tearful performance worthy of an Oscar nomination but Donny successfully begged off the errand. So, Mary Minnis called her best friend next door, and Mama dispatched me. There'd probably be candy money involved.

However, much bigger than a candy bar was the notion that Mama thought I could handle this mission. I ran plenty errands for my mother; no big deal. But this wasn't just running an errand. In my mind, she was asking me to do something another kid couldn't do. It was my first memory of Mama placing in me a certain faith, and it excited me. I didn't want to let her down. I headed next door to the Minnis home, ready for action.

"You gon' run into Busta," a puffy-eyed Donny warned.

"No, I ain't," I snapped, standing in his living room, hands on my ten-year-old hips, like a boy summoned to do a man's job. I could already taste that Butternut, washed down by an ice-cold strawberry Squeeze soda. What'll it be, Mrs. Minnis—cigarettes? half gallon of milk? loaf of bread?

She handed me several dollars and calmly uttered the single word that stopped my adolescent world cold. The request was simple: She needed a box of Kotex.

To paraphrase the Smokey Robinson and the Miracles classic "Tears of a Clown," "There's some sad things known to man/but ain't too much sadder than" (I'll take it from here, Smokey) " . . . sending a boy to the store to buy a box of Kotex."

Like most boys, my early misinformation about life came through the camaraderie of other naive boys. According to those playground geniuses (a) sex was an act always physically painful to girls, (b) a bulletproof vest made a man invincible and (c) Kotex was strictly a girl thing that no young man worth his collection of comics, baseball cards, marbles or pigeons wanted any part of.

Each month without fail, The Box that held the mystery of mysteries would quietly appear unannounced in our bathroom. There it sat for several days, its stark, sixties logo defiantly mum and smirking. And then it would disappear without explanation.

Donny's face filled with horror upon hearing the K word, and he quickly left the room for fear of being wrangled into accompanying me. I pretended I didn't feel the same as he strode out the front door.

I had no problem reaching Safeway. Once inside, I discreetly cased the grocery aisle where Kotex made its home. When that section was free of potential witnesses, I grabbed the box and quickly proceeded to a customer-free checkout counter. Donny's mother had requested the BIG purple box, which not even the biggest brown paper bag could completely conceal.

Though what I carried amounted to Superman's kryptonite, I still remember the immense self-satisfaction that came with having completed the task. You wanna look good in the eyes of your buddy's parents. I'd be a hero in the Minnis household for at least a week.

I'd just put my teeth into that Butternut bar when, just ahead, in the nearly empty parking lot, I set eyes upon Busta and associates. Their eyes followed me the way lions leer at prey just before they pounce. Four older bad guys versus gangly me, armed only with a box of Kotex. No one said life was fair.

"Gimme some money, boy," Busta demanded, standing in my path.

"I ain't got no money."

"I know you got money,' he pressed, " 'cause you just came out the store."

"I ain't got no money," I pleaded. "I just spent it."

Busta wasn't hearing it. "You cain't just come thru here wit' no money for me!" He turned to one of his boys. "*Cut* this lil' motherfucka!"

A henchman's pocketknife was the last thing I saw before jetting across Safeway's parking lot, big purple box of Kotex under my arm and Busta's flunky not far behind. Once past a corner of hedges, I took a sharp right, ducked into Mr. Green's dark, dank garage and prayed that Busta's man hadn't seen where I went. But he did.

I stood petrified in the shadows of a cobwebbed corner, the loud thump of my rapidly beating heart a dead giveaway. "I gotcha now, boy!" The bully thrust his weapon forward into the darkness. I could feel the knife going in. I screamed, and so did my nervous assailant, both of us scared to death to be in the position life had placed us at this very moment. He beat a hasty retreat as I slid slowly down the wall.

Out in the sunlight, it was quiet. No sign of Busta or his gang; only me, staggering in the stillness of a summer afternoon. I was humiliated beyond recognition, but otherwise uninjured. I examined my cumbersome cargo. A small entry hole of about half an inch wide was made by the blade. My childhood dread—a box of Kotex—saved my life.

By the time I returned to Donny's, my tears had dried, my trembling ceased. "You didn't see Busta?" Donny inquired anxiously, figuring I hadn't, since I was standing there in one piece. I simply shook my head. Likewise, the box, dented but true to form, never uttered a word. Mrs. Minnis thanked me for running the errand, gave me fifty cents for my trouble, took the box out of my hands and disappeared into the bathroom.

In the future, being sent off to buy women's sanitary napkins would still amount to cruel and unusual punishment. Admittedly, it would be another couple of years before I'd discover (and fully understand) the true use of its contents. However, from that day forward, I had a lot more respect for the big purple box.

I returned home to considerably less than a hero's welcome—Mama, the minute I walked in the door, instructed me to take out the trash. She never asked how my mission turned out. She didn't have to. The fact that she knew I could do it had me on a cloud for the rest of the day.

SLEIGH RIDE, FIRST CLASS

I WAS FASCINATED with Santa's sleigh.

With four mechanical reindeer "pulling" it, the thing looked like a parade float, though this inquisitive six-year-old suspected that under all that customized design was a flatbed truck equipped with a driver.

The sleigh held about twenty people, who'd sit out in the brisk December air in seats that went along its four sides. As it circled the downtown block, a very live Santa Claus stood in the center of the sleigh, mingling with passengers as a tape of Christmas carols played.

John A. Brown's, one of Oklahoma City's finer department stores in the early sixties, sponsored the ride annually as a holiday attraction for kids with their parents. Mama noticed that I'd been eyeing the contraption from the time she, my three-year-old brother Tony and I got off the city bus on Main Street. So, before we went shopping, we approached the sleigh station.

I wanted badly to ride, but felt out of place. The three of us were the only black people waiting in line, and I noticed several parents and children shooting us disapproving glances. It was a time when Oklahoma City, like most parts of the country, had a hard time seeing blacks as equal. (Only a couple of years ago did I learn that while we stood outside Brown's that day, the store, while accepting black folks' hard-earned money, wouldn't allow them to try on clothes before purchasing them.) At the sleigh station, Mama ignored the uncomfortable reception. "Move on up there," she said, loud enough for other parents in line to hear as she pushed me ahead while carrying Tony on her arm.

Growing up, I never heard Mama speak in terms of color. She wanted her children to know self-respect, but she emphasized our equality by example. Any time we patronized, say, a restaurant, shopping center or any other business on the white side of town, Mama proudly ushered us in with a quiet verve, making it clear to merchants that she expected the same service everyone else got.

Mama allowed Gerald, my oldest brother, sixteen at the time, to join a church group of about sixty adults and youth protesting the banning of blacks from Wedgewood amusement park. I was too young to know what was really happening, but I remember Mama's satisfied smirk as the TV news reported that police had arrested demonstrators at Wedgewood. The only violence associated with the incident occurred when Mama smacked Gerald for saying he bet Martin Luther King, Jr., didn't have to wash dishes at home.

As we climbed aboard his sleigh, Santa, with his rotund belly and a bellowing laugh that sure sounded like the real thing, gave me a wink. Passengers were packed in like sardines. Mama had stern words for a parent about the seating arrangement. "No, we're sitting right here," she said, pointing to a prime spot. I looked up into the mother's fake smile as the little boy, sitting next to me, quietly protested the shoulder of his coat touching mine. Other children, innocent in their ignorance, gaped in curiosity at the brown people. With as many patrons aboard as could find a seat, Santa shut the door to his tacky chariot and we were off.

For the rest of the kids, the ice began to melt as soon as our jolly host began passing out goodies. Decades later, though, I still recall the sensation of feeling invisible after a big, candy-filled stocking making the rounds took a sudden detour before reaching us. It was as if we'd shown up at a party uninvited.

The fat man in the red-and-white suit must have noticed all this. Smiling broadly, he came over and was coaxing me to say my name into the microphone when Bobby Helms's "Jingle Bell Rock" came on. "Oh! I love this song!" he said excitedly. "I need a dance partner!" He looked at my little brother. "Would you like to dance with Santa?" Even as he asked, he was already prying Tony from the arms of my mother. He cradled Tony over his shoulder, took him out into the center of the sleigh and began to dance. I expected my brother to start crying at any moment, but when Santa turned his back to us, there Tony's little round face was, nestled on Santa's shoulder like a diminutive moon, wearing the biggest smile. When I looked up at Mama she seemed tickled at how much both Tony and Santa seemed to be enjoying themselves. A mother and her three kids at the other end of the sleigh began to clap to the music, and soon more joined in.

Kids still stared, their curiosity replaced, I now imagine by admiration and envy. After all, when you're a child, you can't do too much better than have a personal relationship with Santa Claus. When the song ended, the whole sleigh applauded. My shyness was replaced by an overwhelming sense of pride.

We were the last passengers to disembark. As we did so, Mama stopped to have a word with Santa. I couldn't hear what she said, but it was in a tone direct yet cordial. Through the fake beard I saw a smile. The lilt of his words to Mama was friendly and respectful. Suddenly, he didn't sound like a Santa Claus at all, but just a regular ol' man who was happy to make a family comfortable in spite of circumstances.

What a difference one fake-sleigh ride can make. We left the dock as nonentities in someone's eyes and returned, whether or not every passenger approved, as first-class citizens. Mama, with help from Santa, saw to it.

MODEL BEHAVIOR

MY CLASSMATES in group 2 had a good laugh when, after everyone in our fifth-grade class finished pulling names out of a box, they learned I'd be exchanging Christmas gifts with Nathaniel Brunswick.

They used to tease Lil' Nate, as he was called in the neighborhood, for his b.b. buckshot naps and a tendency toward oversized clothes, the result of sharing a tattered wardrobe with seven older brothers and sisters. Miss Florence, Nate's hard-working mom and a single parent who squeezed her family into a small, ramshackle two-bedroom home just off Eighth Street on Oklahoma City's black East Side, not far from where I lived.

The slight, soft-spoken Nate stayed to himself, but was funny and inquisitive if you got to know him. A fast runner, during gym period everyone wanted him on their relay team. Otherwise, he was mostly on his own.

According to Mrs. Long, our teacher, the gift giving would take place in shifts: One week, half the class would give gifts; the next week, the givers would be on the receiving end.

"You not gon' get nothin' from Nate," Charles Whitmore declared, doubling over in laughter. "His family is so poor they eatin' bread and water."

"No, he'll get something," disagreed Clara Parkins, sounding sympathetic before busting up with, "Somebody's hand-me-downs!"

I laughed along with them, but it wasn't funny. I wasn't thinking about Nate, who sat back in group 3 with more than a notion we were discussing him; I was worried how it would look to the class if I didn't get anything.

"That's not your problem," Mama said that evening as she prepared dinner. "You just do your part." She told me to go get her purse, then reached into it and dispatched me to TG&Y around the corner. After playing with my share of merchandise in the toy section, I remembered Nate speaking proudly about his "Invisible Daddy," as Whitmore used to taunt—a man who seldom came around but whom Nate loved to recall drove a "cherry red Chevy Impala. With skirts." I settled on just such a model car—a '65 Chevy Impala—and a tube of glue.

Mama wrapped the five-dollar gift to look like a million bucks, her craftsmanship ignored Friday morning by Nate as he quickly tore open the package at his desk. Trying not to blush only makes it more pronounced. From my desk I could see Nate mouthing "Impala" to himself as he examined all sides of the box, checking out the pictures.

At school, Nate's gratitude was cordial. However, when Miss Florence called to thank Mama, she described a child in a state of rapture. She said Nate planned to assemble the car and present it to the Invisible Daddy. "You'd think we gave that boy a bicycle," Mama remarked, as she hung up the phone. Gingerly inquiring whether Miss Florence had mentioned a gift for me only instigated a scolding. "Stevie, they barely got money for food," Mama said. "Let's just be happy you could give."

I sought solace in Mama's words as I moped into Mrs. Long's class the following Friday, to no avail. It wasn't about a present, really. I simply didn't want to come up empty in front of my friends. I ventured to the gift table with the rest of them purely as a contrived show of faith. But there, in the center of the table, wrapped as if it were worth a million bucks, was a package with my name on it.

After defiantly waving it in the faces of Whitmore and Parkins, I went to my desk and tried to be cool as I tore through Santa Claus wrapping. In a shoe box, newspaper stuffing parted to reveal a toy car. Not just any car—a model Impala, assembled so seamlessly that it seemed held together not by glue, but love. In the box was a note written in typical fifth-grade scribble: "DeAr StePhen. I PainTed It Red. I Hope YOu LikE Red. MeRRy ChriSTmas NaThANiel BruNsWicK."

While my friends oohed and aahed, I looked over my shoulder at Nate. He kept his eyes straight ahead at first, ignoring me until I made his eyes find mine. I smiled and held up the red Impala, and he returned a smile that was wide and proud. And just a little pained.

That evening, Mama and I bundled up and walked the few blocks to Nate's house to return the red Impala. I didn't see why I had to give it back, but she mentioned something about a lesson in it all that I wouldn't truly grasp until later in life.

Mama was right. I will never forget the expression on Nate's face when he turned on his porch light to find me standing under it, clutching that shoe box. Giving has a certain power about it.

WHO MAMA WAS

SEVERAL YEARS BACK, during a phone conversation, my "little" brother Kevin—who, with a wife and children and weighing more than me, isn't little at all—asked me about our mother.

He doesn't really remember Mama, which I've always found interesting, considering that he used to be her shadow. How strange it must be for him to look at the photograph of himself as a small child, with this tall, lean, bespectacled woman.

Your brothers and sister have undoubtedly told you plenty about our mama, Kevin. Now it's my turn.

A couple of days before the first Mother's Day that I can remember, Mama gave me money to buy her a handkerchief at TG&Y, helped me wrap it and then on Mother's Day reacted as if she'd been presented the Hope diamond. That's who Mama was. She taught us things by having us do them, and treated whatever good we did as if it was something truly remarkable.

When any of her kids participated in school events, Mama was quietly on the scene, smiling. She would go to PTA meetings in the evening and bring home whatever snacks they had—finger sandwiches and pastel colored mints—for us to munch on.

Mama wore red lipstick.

When our brother Tony had to be hospitalized for something or another, Mama listened intently to what the doctors said they were going to do, and then she told them what they were going to do. Back home, she'd bravely report the events of her hospital visit to Daddy and then break down and cry.

Mama drank at least two cups of coffee in the morning and smoked Viceroy brand cigarettes.

Kevin, Mama was a conventional woman with an inquisitive nature for the unconventional. Although she was Baptist, she kept a jar of Catholic holy water in the hall closet. She was mild-mannered and low-key. I don't remember her saying anything racist or unduly mean-spirited. Mama wasn't a saint, but I don't think you will find a better mother.

We wanted whatever Mama had. After we begged like baby chicks, she would tease, "Can I, can I, can I! If I were eating poison, would you want that, too?" To which we'd meekly reply, "Yes."

Mama could cook. She could fry chicken, bake bread, cakes and pies, and make candy from scratch. When Mama went grocery shopping at Safeway, she always took the same route in the store, starting in the produce section and ending in the bread aisle. In a pinch, with no facilities in sight, Mama could always find a place for us boys to pee.

One of Mama's favorite songs was Percy Sledge's "When a Man Loves a Woman." Her favorite "stories," as daytime dramas were called back then, were *As the World Turns* and the ominously titled *Edge of Night*.

Once a week, Mama sought to numb the pain of her life with alcohol, gin being her preference.

After some years as a housewife and then working as Dr. Porter's housekeeper, Mama put herself through college and got a degree in child development, all while working at a day care and raising a family. I imagine the books and classes were a mere formality.

When we'd run you out of our bedroom, we knew we had to capture you before you got down the hall and made that quick right, because Mama's room was the demilitarized zone, and you were her heart. Some might have characterized your arrival in the Ivory household as "late," but for Mama, you were right on time. She was simply enamored with you.

Despite many Mother's Days without her, Mama is still with us, because we are her. Certain qualities that you cannot explain—the way you shift your body when you stand, or purse your lips when you concentrate on something; your willingness to speak to strangers, your sense of manners or just your general inclination to want to do the right thing—these things have an origin.

This is who Mama was.

DADDY'S
FREEING WORDS

THE POSTER FOR **COLORS**, the gritty 1988 drama about Los Angeles gang culture starring Sean Penn and Robert Duvall, reads: TWO COPS. TWO GANGS. ONE HELL OF A WAR. Mentioned nowhere in the hype is what I personally consider the movie's most compelling element: my daddy, John Ivory.

Thanks to my brother Gerald, a probation officer and gang authority who was a consultant on the film, my father spent a day as a *Colors* film extra. Daddy is the stocky man with the shaven head standing front and center in the church scene during a gang member's funeral, peering, to the distress of director Dennis Hopper, directly into the camera.

According to Gerald, Hopper shot several takes of the scene, each time gingerly reminding Daddy that he wasn't to look into the camera. However, the shout of "Action!" time and again lured his eyes into the lens. Finally, Hopper said to hell with it and just left the scene in.

That John Ivory is somewhere on a reel with the likes of Duvall and Penn simply personifies who he is—a simple man from Winfield, Louisiana, who yet somehow always seems to have an all-access backstage pass.

He had a postman gig at Tinker Air Force Base and in the evenings and on weekends served as chief bartender at the base Officers' Club. Though Daddy retired almost twenty years ago, he still treats the base as his personal domain, going, as he did when he worked there, damn near anywhere he wants. The terms "off limits" and "top secret" never applied to him.

Members of my family saw the stealth bomber before much of the public knew it existed; Daddy drove his car right out on the tarmac into a secure area and said, "I want to show this to some people." When the guards saw that the intruder was John Ivory—legendary bartender from the Tinker Officers' Club whose glad-handing with multistar generals and other high-level military types got the bar officially christened by placard, ceremony and all, the Ivory Room—they went at ease and said, "Sure, John." It was the kind of gumption that made me, as a child, see my Daddy as a god.

While he's always greeted friends and strangers alike with his trademark "Whatdaya say, there," often while putting a hurting on a stick of gum, Daddy's all-access backstage pass didn't take him too many places emotionally.

The man I remember came in from a job every day at a certain time, stripped to his boxers, read the evening paper and occupied the couch in front of the TV for much of the evening, gazing at *Cheyenne* and *The Untouchables*.

Daddy was much like the daddies of my childhood friends'—hard, often physical laborers who mostly left the sensitive side of parenting to their wives, checking in when discipline was due.

Not to say Daddy wasn't fun. On the weekend Mama would prepare a bag of popcorn and a thermos of grape Kool-Aid and send us off with Daddy to the Twilight Gardens Drive-in for Godzilla movies.

In the mid-sixties, long before Mama's passing, Daddy took my younger brother Tony and me to our first concert, a breathtaking revelation called the James Brown Revue, at Douglass High School's football stadium. When we got older, he treated us to so-called blaxploitation flicks, indulging en route in intermittent philosophical discussions that always began with a wistful "Son, *whatever* you do in life . . ."

The affection I recall between him and Mama consisted of my occasionally waking up in his arms in the middle of the night as he carried me out of the room where they slept, putting me in bed with my brothers, returning to her and closing the door behind him.

However, I'd say the love between my parents was pretty much gone by my arrival. He and Mama, between working and raising a family, drifted apart emotionally. Some evenings, Daddy didn't come home. We kids made Mama aware of a growing number of hang-up calls coming to the house. They were divorced before my teens, and Mama was left with the day-to-day job of parenting. When she passed, Daddy, to the fluster of his current wife, returned home to finish raising the three boys left at home from a brood of five.

He came back at a time when I, a rebellious, introverted teenager and the oldest of the three, despised The Man, The System, and the fact that, without a mother, my life lay at the mercy of Daddy. I now saw him as a simple man who didn't know much about anything beyond putting food on the table. And I resented his thinking he'd just come back and be Daddy.

That first year was filled with disputes, defiance, Daddy's earnest but dubious attempts at cooking—his specialty being weenie omelets and anything with "Helper" on the box—and my ill-engineered plots to run away. It all climaxed with the first Mother's Day after Mama's death.

Daddy went out and got white carnations, symbolic on Mother's Day of the loss of one's mother. I deemed the idea conventional, conforming and corny. I wasn't going to church and was definitely not wearing a carnation. During the various stages of putting on their Sunday best, Tony and Kevin looked at me, incredulous that I wasn't getting dressed.

Eventually, I did don my cheap little suit, but when Daddy finally said, "C'mon, Stevie," I countered with a trembling, "Daddy, I'm not going," after which he collared me—you wrinkled my shirt, Daddy—which scared me so that I promptly peed my pants, and backhanded me across my face. Not anything that hurt, just enough to demonstrate who was boss. We sat in the front pew of the first church Daddy came to, me wearing a white carnation and urine and praying that my pants might dry before we had to walk out of there. After that Mother's Day, a line was drawn: No matter what I thought of my father, he was my father, and my notions of rebellion were best left to the pouty white kids I watched on TV situation comedies; Daddy wasn't having it.

However, obeying Daddy didn't mean I believed he was sensitive and intuitive enough to know who I really was inside. Thus, I was surprised that he would utter to me some of the most important words of my life. They were words inspired by a call from a high school counselor, who told him if his son didn't stop cutting classes, he wasn't going to graduate.

Something like this would usually get Daddy shouting. This time, though, he calmly called me into his room and sat me down on what will always be Mama's bed. From the mouth and heart of a man whom I'd seen cry only maybe twice in my life emerged words that soothed like tender poetry to a black-sheep middle son. "Son," he began wearily, rubbing his bald head, "out of all my kids, you're the one I just don't . . . understand."

What came after that, I don't recall. Doesn't matter, anyway. Suddenly—finally—I had an explanation as to why I shied away from playing sports and hanging out with the fellas, why I listened to the Beatles when others were listening to the Temptations and why I was a seventeen-year-old virgin when most of my buddies weren't. I was . . . different, given permission to be so by the one person I didn't think perceptive enough to know his third child that way.

A child's relationship with his parents can be a roller coaster of emotions. When we are young, they are our heroes. Then we get older and realize they are mortal. Sometimes, children need to know that parents themselves understand that they don't have all the answers. That admission alone can change everything.

That talk forever altered my relationship with Daddy. It allowed me to see him as more than just the man who went back and forth to work, sometimes without saying more than a sentence beyond instruction regarding chores. He was paying attention to us, paying attention to me. Because of this, Daddy's words did something else: They gave me permission to be me.

I did graduate, and not simply from high school. By the time I left home for Los Angeles, I appreciated my father in a way that I never knew I could—for being the person I never knew he was.

PART III

IN THE BEGINNING, THERE WAS AWKWARD

LAJUAN HAWKINS, LADIES' MAN

JO ANNE MILLER was nodding off. Undoubtedly one of the smartest, cutest and most popular girls in my ninth-grade class, Jo Anne was usually quick to raise her hand or go to the blackboard. Today, she was uncharacteristically restless and preoccupied. From the rear of the classroom that was a slackers' haven, I observed Jo Anne, knowing her dilemma was summed up in two words: LaJuan Hawkins.

Jo Anne had been on the phone with him all night.

For the second evening in a row, she'd been caught up in a dizzying, euphoric haze of puppy love, as they talked about school, about the latest records and TV shows, about Ronnie Sullivan's crazy daddy and about the mechanics of kissing. By midnight, Jo Anne was only the latest girl at Oklahoma City's F. D. Moon Junior High to fall under the spell of LaJuan Hawkins. LaJuan was tall, lean and sexy, his baby face framed by a hip, shoulder-length Afro fashionable in an era ruled by the Jackson 5 and the Brady Bunch. He was also a junior high school girl's dream: a cool senior from another school. He spent weekends at house parties, hung out at the mall till all hours and made defiant lunchtime appearances at schools outside his district.

Neither his picture nor his name was in the yearbook of Northeast High—the school he was said to attend on the city's upwardly mobile integrated part of town. But then, LaJuan wasn't on anyone's radar.

None of the girls with whom he regularly communicated by phone in Moon Junior High's upper echelon—smart, good-looking girls, pretty majorettes, curvy cheerleaders from bourgeois families—had ever laid eyes on LaJuan, even though he told them he frequented some of their favorite places. In fact, no kid on the city's predominantly black East Side, boy or girl, was familiar with LaJuan.

Nobody, that is, except me.

The fast friendship between a cool, elusive high school senior with good looks and a running car and a gangly, invisible nerd who spent his weekends sitting at home listening to Top 40 radio and watching *Mutual of Omaha's Wild Kingdom* might have seemed unlikely. But in fact, both LaJuan and I were loners who refused to bow to a clique. We were outsiders and proud of it. In certain ways, the ways that counted, we were distinctively alike: We both refused to participate in our respective physical education classes, and neither of us got involved in any of our school's extracurricular activities, including cheesy cafeteria school dances and the like. What difference did it make if LaJuan chose not to participate and I simply wasn't invited? The result was the same.

In any case, word of my camaraderie with LaJuan spread quickly, making me, to the chagrin of some of the more popular fellas, the new best friend of some of the finest girls in school.

Seldom was the chatter about me; it was all about LaJuan. I didn't mind. After all, LaJuan was one incredible guy—everything I wanted to be. For one thing, unlike me, Hawkins knew just what to say to the ladies. The hard heads that I knew would finally get a girl on the phone and want to gab about sports or cars; LaJuan's calls were subdued, intense productions of adolescent sensuality.

He'd do more listening than talking, but when he did speak, his soothing man-child voice, often carried along by the strategically faint strains of Stevie Wonder or the Stylistics, would pierce the still of a squirming girl's dark bedroom, creating lusty havoc. Princess phone lines were scorched, hearts effectively taken.

Pretty soon some of the guys around Moon Junior High had grown impatient with the very idea of LaJuan. He was all a growing number of their female classmates wanted to talk about. In study hall, bravado was spewed about actually forming a posse and heading over to Northeast and seeking out the mystery teen who had so enthralled their women.

The fellas were spared having to back up such big talk: One Thursday night, LaJuan's career as a Romeo came unceremoniously crashing down, by his own hand, no less.

Looking back, it was all wrong from the beginning. This particular evening, LaJuan, usually fixated with homecoming queens and pom-pom girls, was on the phone with the sweet but decidedly unpopular Patricia Edgeworth—more my type than LaJuan's. But there he was in Patricia's ear, Smokey and the Miracles providing the sultry backdrop, his usually fatal second gear of red-hot nothings was intercepted by the words: "STEVIE, IT'S AFTER TEN, GET OFF THE PHONE!"

That very instant, for about five excruciating seconds in 1970, the earth stopped turning (there is no need to check with anyone on this; it happened, trust me), its rotation halted, for the first time in the history of the world, by stark, reputation-curdling silence.

The only thing heard throughout the immediate galaxy was Smokey's recorded pleading, "Baby, baby, don't cry. . . ," the sound of Patricia's widening eyes and her heart-crushing disappointment. I quickly hung up the phone—but not before Patricia got to hear me frantically answer my perplexed mother in the suave, debonair, *nervous* voice of LaJuan.

In an exhibition of mercy of biblical proportions, Patricia Edgeworth did not reveal my pitiful little secret. Three days after my last deed of deception—the face-saving news to LaJuan's heartbroken stable that the fashionably antiwar Hawkins had abruptly joined the army—she phoned me.

Patricia conceded that she almost told Hawkins devotee Eva Jackson that I was LaJuan, but decided against it. She then broke a moment of awkward, typically teenage phone silence by asking if I, of all people, would be her partner on the plant project in Mr. Oliver's biology class.

A quivering yes, the runoff of my flabbergasted glee, was all I could muster. As it turned out, pea plants in milk cartons would not be the only specimen sprouting in biology class that semester. Through an amalgamation of fate and chemistry, I discovered romance a science unto itself, self being the natural active element. Good-bye, LaJuan Hawkins; hello, me.

THE DIVINE AFFECTION OF SISTER ELAINE

I **COULDN'T HANG OUT** with the fellas after school; I had to get home. It was Wednesday and that meant my weekly visit from Sister Elaine.

I joined the Catholic faith on my own, with Mama's blessing, when I was fifteen. It was my sister, Barbara, who actually sparked my exodus, when she invited Sister Elizabeth and Sister Elaine in off the porch one evening as they went door to door recruiting.

I'd read Barbara's catechism, the official how-to-be-a-Catholic study guide, with a zeal usually reserved for comics and cheap sci-fi novels, fascinated by matter-of-fact details about each of us being assigned a guardian angel and about Purgatory, a kind of after-death holding tank for sinners who do time before going on to Heaven. I decided to study and become Catholic.

In my little universe, it was a big deal for me to break away from the time-honored tradition of the Baptist Church. Generally speaking, if you were black, you were Baptist or something sufficiently dramatic. Religion aside, my belief was that to go Catholic was to go up-town, with genteel, liberal white folks and bourgeois blacks. The music wasn't much, but you didn't have to get dressed up. Sunday mass—civil, linear and without emotion—was over in about an hour.

Sister Elaine, my perpetually pleasant tutor, stood five foot nothing with sparkling blue eyes magnified by round granny specs that sat on a turned-up nose. Her middle age was probably not as old as I perceived at the time. She was female, however, and for the hour or so a week that we studied, there in my living room, I judiciously fought the battle of good versus evil.

There was something about Sister's uncompromising goodness that distinctly turned me on. I could ask her virtually anything, and no matter how stupid it rang, she would listen intently and, always smiling, answer my query as best she could. As she serenely went about the day's Bible lesson, I wondered just what went on under that drab, ankle-length dark blue habit: When was the last time sunlight hit her pale skin, and why, if her outfit was about dissuading lustful feelings, had it failed me? I'd sit there, imagining her saintly uniform concealed the unrelenting, bodacious body of an Ikette.

It is easy to understand how children would be susceptible to the despicable deeds of preying religious figures; at this age, we are most impressionable about life events as crucial as God and sex. In my early teens, I read both the catechism and *Penthouse* "Forum" letters, well, religiously.

As a result, every Saturday afternoon at nearby Corpus Christi Church, I'd make my way into the confessional booth. Topping my shortlist would be the one infraction most common among boys my age.

It's been said that dog is man's best friend. No offense to Lassie, Rin Tin Tin, Krypto, Scooby Doo, firehouse mascots and all great dogs, famous and anonymous, but I'd say dog is man's *second* most vital comrade; his first in his hand.

I don't remember exactly when I discovered masturbation, but when I did, it was a good day. Suddenly, there was a way to bring to wondrous conclusion my dizzying episodes of sexual arousal. It was empowering;

I could do this alone. For free. It quickly became my favorite thing.

I'd glean plenty of inspiration for my joy sessions from the eye candy in the school hallways. However, television was really it for me. Alone in my room, I'd peruse the dial in search of a lover. Variety shows with high-kicking dance ensembles were usually a good source of excitement. I used to tear Lola Falana up when she was on Bill Cosby's comedy hour. *The Partridge Family*'s Susan Dey was too skinny and pretty David Cassidy a dude, but Mama Partridge, curvy Shirley Jones, did the trick. I slept with all the *Price Is Right* girls (in my fantasies). Had the TV remote existed back then, I probably wouldn't be alive today, dead from exhaustion.

Still, it was Sister Elaine who provoked my most illicit thoughts. Sometimes it's what you can't see that excites, and Sister, covered from head to toe, drove me wild. Through the confessional's concealing partition, I'd whisper with anguished austerity the usual, "Forgive me, Father, for I have sinned. It has been one week since my last confession," and on cue, Father Folken, on the other side, would sigh as if to say, "Yeah, yeah, yeah, look, kid, you're going to go blind if you keep this up."

Like a doctor prescribing a stronger pill, each Saturday he'd tack on a few more Hail Marys for me to recite as penance. I'd always exit the confessional thinking that for the penalty of masturbation, I could have had real sex.

I don't know how I found the nerve to confess my feelings to Sister Elaine, but at the close of a lesson I managed to get out of my mouth, "I . . . I think I am in love with you." Not altogether surprised, Sister looked thoughtfully at the fifteen-year-old before her and smiled.

"Well, I could say that I love you, too," she said, putting her lesson books in her bag. "And I do, but I know you mean something different."

She gingerly explained that for a man and woman to truly love in the romantic sense is a gift from God that involves mutual respect, communication, dedication and personal responsibility. The only loves more important, Sister said, are those of God and self.

"It's not like what you see on TV or in the movies," she cautioned. With Him in their lives, however, a couple would be able to weather any life challenge. The more they endured together, the greater their love for each other.

I wondered how a woman with no man could know so much about that kind of love. I wanted no part of what she'd described. Sounded like work. I was simply looking for someone to . . . talk to or listen to music with. Not even for sex, the reality of which scared me to death.

"Well," I finally said begrudgingly, "I *do* know what love is, and I love you."

"I love you, too," said Sister.

In the weight of the moment I looked away from her, but when I glanced back a second later, her eyes still held a wistful gaze off somewhere, as if what she said had sparked a memory.

My infatuation with Catholicism wouldn't officially end until early adulthood. Dissension was sparked by something I'd read in my catechism early on that silently nagged me throughout my brief Catholic tenure—the idea that Catholicism was the one and only true religion, and that everything else, no matter how ambitious, was moot. Even as a child, it occurred to me that God could never be so rigid in His thinking when there seemed to exist so many sincere roads to His love. The Catholic Church's unyielding position on this, along with a hankering to explore other forms of spiritual expression, made me let go.

However, my respect and appreciation of the experience remain, and I've often wondered, if I were still there, would the newspaper headlines regarding the abuse of power by Catholic priests shake my dedication.

Undoubtedly, I'd turn to the kind and ever faithful Sister Elaine, and hope she could explain it all.

THE BOY WHO COULDN'T CLOSE

EVEN IF WE DIDN'T have a very conventional relationship, Rhonda Logan was my girl-friend.

I met her during my senior year at Douglass High. She was a junior. We spent plenty of time on the phone, but never saw each other outside school for so much as a hamburger. The lack of a car or license to drive one kept us from the relationship I dreamed of, or so I told myself.

More likely, I was scared to death. Rhonda was tall

and caramel-colored, with big brown eyes, a cute nose and a big soft, brown Afro. When she put on all that makeup and those hoop earrings, she resembled a living doll. I couldn't figure why such a good-natured, soft-spoken girl would be interested in me.

That didn't stop me from bragging about her, though. I was holding court one day with the fellas in physical education class—in the bleachers, of course, where all us guys who didn't dress for P.E. lounged—when the impish Ernest Hollingsworth rained on my parade.

"Have you closed yet?" he asked.

"Huh?"

"You heard me. You up here sayin' she's your girl-friend and all—have you closed the deal?"

Hollingsworth's daddy worked for a downtown car dealership, and Ernest thought sales jargon was cool. I knew what he was asking. I told him it wasn't any of his business.

"Then you answered my question, Ivory."

I thought of Hollingsworth as my flight touched down at Oklahoma City's Will Rogers World Airport, home for summer after my first year of college in Los Angeles.

Rhonda needed to know I was a different man than the boy who left OKC. I'd seen tings, baby: lived in a town with where city buses ran *all night;* where they had more than one black music radio station, and they broadcast all night, too, as opposed to the dusk-till-dawn jive to which Oklahoma City's KBYE was regulated; where people ate something called an avocado and where even folk in the ghetto pronounced some words properly. Hey, I lived just a couple of freeway exits from Disneyland.

I wouldn't tell her that this country boy still didn't have a car. Most important, she could never know that of the things I'd shaken in California, one thing made the trip with me to L.A. and back: my virginity.

When I saw Rhonda again, she had a quaint little single apartment, an old Mustang and a job that required a white uniform and white stockings, either at a doctor's office or a soda fountain, I forget which. Moreover, I noticed that she had somehow . . . changed. On the summer nights that we sat under the stars in front of my family's house or visited the hot and happening Dairy Queen on NW Twenty-third, I'd sense from her a restless maturity not revealed in our letters and sporadic long-distance phone calls.

We spent our final afternoon together looking at daytime TV. The vibe was thicker than the humidity in the air from the air conditioner rattling in Rhonda's apartment window. I felt a bit out of control of the situation. She lay on her bed in silent anticipation, dressed for work but hoping I'd make a move, her occasional frustrated sigh seeming to say, "Boy, you better come on; soon I'll be at work taking a patient's blood pressure"— or scooping Rocky Road—"and we're both going to be sorry."

Aflame with quiet desire but crippled by shyness, I sat next to her bed making nervous banter, measuring eternity in thirty-minute TV time blocks. I'd wasted weeks on hand-holding and the like, and now it was down to a few hours before she was to be at work and I'd head back to L.A. I was almost twenty-one; I would *not* go back to Los Angeles a virgin, damn it. I just wouldn't. *Let's Make A Deal* came on and host Monty Hall's lingo reminded me of Hollingsworth's taunting words and my mission: *I . . . must . . . close.*

At exactly 2:25 P.M., as Hall introduced the Big Deal of the Day, I slowly reached for Rhonda's hand. With a distressed smile, she gripped it tightly. . . .

Later at the airport, I imagined the airline ticket clerk politely asking, "And will you be checking your virginity in with the rest of your luggage or carrying it on board?" Either way, I was leaving Oklahoma City an unchanged man. Sometimes, young men pursue things for all the wrong reasons.

I'd return to a world of Disneyland and avocados,

still burdened with my virginity. As for Rhonda, she went, hopefully, into the arms of someone who wouldn't attempt to make love to a woman for the first time thirty minutes before she had to be at work.

If I ever see Hollingsworth again in this life, I'll choke him.

THE NOISY EMANCIPATION OF VIRGIN MAN

ON THE MORNING CITY bus en route to City College, Smokey Robinson's new hit "Virgin Man" was again haunting me.

The guy holding the radio derived particular glee from the part that said, "It ain't like I never wanted to/but it's easier to think than it is to do." He thought that so funny. The snickering passenger didn't know that three seats away sat a young man for whom Robinson's tune was a private anthem.

The worldly attire—navy denim bell-bottoms, platform boots, wild, Hendrix-after-taxes Afro and cool, miniature spoon dangling from the neck of a naive Oklahoma boy who would only later discover its connection to cocaine—concealed a secret identity: In the early seventies, at age twenty, I *was* Virgin Man.

For almost twenty years, I'd heard stories of after-school "trains"; witnessed used, dried-up condoms carried in wallets like trophies and displayed as manhood's evidence; read *Penthouse* "Forum" letters and heard braggarts insist how satisfied they'd left their partners. But for me that particular line from Smokey's song was true. To a boy who'd yet to experience sex, "Virgin Man" seemed like sheer exploitation in the hands of Smokey, whose looks and celebrity had undoubtedly afforded him plenty of sex in this life. Besides, if someone had to recite their sagas of sexuality, someone had to listen. Unbearably shy and inexperienced in the ways of love, I figured that, for the foreseeable future, that would be my job.

Until Danielle.

We met on campus. About five foot seven, lean and attractive in an artsy way, Danielle was slightly older. She had a job, an apartment, a car and an attraction to me, even though, living with my aunt Jewel, I had none of those things.

Long campus chats morphed into long walks in

the park and beachside frolicking. When I found my-self on her couch one evening after class, I didn't know what dizzied me more, her kisses or the cheap sherry.

She turned me on to jazz-fusion. With Return to Forever's "Where Have I Known You Before" supply-ing the musical backdrop, I had a revelation. A couple, actually. One: If a young man thinketh too much—no matter how excited, healthy and virile—when the mo-ment of truth arrives, his equipment will suddenly let him . . . down.

The more significant discovery was just how patient and loving a woman could be. For weeks, Danielle nur-tured me as if I was anything but a man with the Erec-tion of Life that waned when I reached her bed. I didn't tell her I'd never done any of this before, and she never asked. It was as close as I'd come to unconditional love from someone not of kin.

Or perhaps Danielle simply knew something I didn't. For one Friday evening, a muted bedroom TV our only light, a hunger came over me that foreplay could not spook. I lay on top of her, and it began. She softly asked me how I was doing, and that was the last I saw of the woman I'd previously known.

I felt Danielle slowly lose herself in me. Later in life I'd come to envy this—a woman's ability to perfectly lose herself this way—and that evening, I reveled in sensations I'd never imagined. I thought of all the stories I'd endured, all the issues of *Swank, Gent* and *Nugget* I'd perused to find this moment. I thought of poor Adam in that Garden. I had a whole new understanding. And sympathy.

My thoughts were interrupted by Danielle.

"There it is," she said somewhat deliriously, under her breath.

There *what* is? I wondered. Before I could make a fool of myself by asking, she said it again, first with a breathy urgency before nearly cracking my eardrum: "There it is . . . there it is . . . there it is . . . THERE IT IS, THERE IT IS, THERE IT IS, THERE IT IS, THERE IT IS, THERE IT IS, THERE IT IS, DON'T STOP, THERE IT IS, THAT'S IT, THERE IT FUCKING IS! ! ! AARGHHHHHHHHHHHHHH! !" That instant, someone next door knocked on the wall, which made Danielle's dog start barking.

Danielle went limp and burst out crying. When she finally opened her eyes, she found me atop her, my eyes as wide as saucers, gaping in terror. I asked her if I'd hurt her. She just smiled and sighed, "No, baby"—she said "baby" as if she were a mother gently consoling her child—"that was *supposed* to happen." Answering the door in her robe, she had some choice words for the apartment manager, who said there was a report that a murder was being committed in #303.

Danielle taught me the distinct differences between sex and love, and the intimate features of both. I'd been shy and a virgin, but I was a more-than-willing student.

THE WORD ACCORDING TO MISS FINE

WELL, HELLO, STRANGER."

It had been years, but I remembered the voice. The tangy tone and pleasant lilt now held a certain maturity, but it still belonged to Bobbi Banks, or as we called her in high school, Miss Fine.

Pure, unadulterated sex on platform boots, Bobbi dated bad boys with beat-up Impalas who would pick her up after school. However, unlike most of the high school's hip and happening, Bobbi wasn't snooty. In sixth period, she actually used to talk to me. It was the only reason I went to class, to be near those dangerous curves.

But by 1985 that seemed like a lifetime ago. We were both thirty and in different worlds. Bobbi was in Oklahoma City, divorced and employed by the city, and I was in L.A. working as a writer. She'd gotten my number from our old classmate Harrison Knight, whom she ran into at Montgomery Ward. She hoped I didn't mind her calling; she just wanted to say hello. I was pleasantly stunned.

After some small talk, Bobbi said she had to go, but gave me her number and invited me to phone later. I counted the hours, and that night, during an intoxicating eight-hour call, we did the dance. There was laughter and flirting and sighs and lapses of sexy silence. And, a confession: Bobbi Banks, the girl I used to fantasize about walking hand in hand with into the local Dairy Queen after school, would have dated me—acute shyness and all-—if I'd only asked. By dawn, we'd both decided to get reacquainted. A trip back home planned long before Bobbi's call was suddenly redefined into a nerd's revenge.

Several weeks and phone calls later, standing in the lobby of the Oklahoma City Radisson Hotel, I was nervous. What if the Bobbi picking me up for dinner wasn't the Bobbi I remembered in school? Infinitely worse, what if who she finds standing here is still the guy I remember myself to be back in school—someone who could never have a chance in hell with a girl like Miss Fine?

Maturity somehow seems to have it in for celebrities and the subjects of childhood crushes; generally, neither fare well under the physical demands of time. But as a striding Bobbi stopped hotel lobby traffic, it was clear that adulthood agreed with her. Stunning in a shoulder-length bob and a subtly accessorized, formfitting white linen skirt that showcased those long legs, she had gotten better, if that was possible. And if she was disappointed with what she saw, she didn't show it, thank God. In a restaurant as cozy, charming and Italian as could be found in a town big on steak houses, I found she was funny, well-read, forward-thinking, sexy as hell and something else I couldn't put my finger on. The red wine worked well in navigating us through our giddy uneasiness, and ultimately, back to my hotel room.

While Bobbi excused herself to the bathroom, I frantically toiled to transform a weekend-rate hotel room into a love den. I turned down the lamp a notch and opened the curtains to transform the huge, bright gas station sign across the street into a love light. I found the lone R&B station on the radio dial, and pulled back the bedding just so, strategically placing a couple of condoms under one of the pillows. Kicking off her shoes and sitting on the edge of the bed when she emerged from the bathroom, Bobbi softly said the conversation earlier was great, but she had unfinished business. In my best Barry White tone, I said I did, too. And then, before I could say anything more, Bobbi Banks kissed me.

It started slowly, with just the lips, and then I felt her tongue snake into my mouth. It was a deep, passionate, mind-blowing kiss, a kiss about a decade overdue. I closed my eyes. God bless Harrison Knight. I couldn't tell my date that I was about to finally, unbelievably, settle up on years of nervous, horny teen nerdism.

Her soft cheek against mine, Bobbi whispered into my ear that she had a gift for me, something she wanted to climb through the phone and share during all our late-night long-distance conversations, and certainly over dinner, but dared not, lest I got the wrong idea.

"I guarantee you, baby," I whispered, "I'm not gonna get the wrong idea."

I opened my eyes to find, sitting on those tight, bronze thighs, an open Bible.

"Jesus, Bobbi . . ."

"Then you know Him?"

"Well . . . *yeah*, but . . ."

Bobbi explained that after being lied to by one too

many men in her life, several years ago she'd given herself to the Man Upstairs. She said she often dreamed of the quiet guy she used to sit next to in sixth period. She fantasized that he would one day return to Oklahoma to share her life, but when he finally arrived, she realized over dinner that the guy deserved to chase his own dream instead. And then she turned to a scripture about friendship.

As Bobbi read aloud by the light of the gas station sign over faint strains of the Dramatics, I might have actually shed a tear. Not just for Bobbi and me, but for misguided former nerds and misunderstood sex goddesses all over the world.

IN SEARCH
OF A LIE,
I FOUND THE TRUTH

IT WAS ENGINE COOLANT that finally woke me up. But by then it was too late.

The year was 1980. I was twenty-five years old and deeply in love. At least that is what I called it.

No matter what I thought it was, six months into our relationship, when my girlfriend told me she wouldn't see me that evening—that Friday night she'd be having a drink with The Girls—I became concerned. My girlfriend at the time, you have to understand, was a champion flirt. We'd met, in fact, during one of her after-work forays with this very group of man-eaters.

By eight o'clock that evening, after I'd phoned several times and got no answer, I got a sinking feeling. When her car still wasn't in the stall behind her apartment building by eleven, I became thoroughly convinced that whenever she did return, she would not be alone.

A hunch wasn't enough, however. I needed to witness this act of infidelity with my own eyes.

So, in what I saw as a remarkable feat of domestic surveillance, I slid myself under Miss Parkinson's gray 1967 Buick Skylark, two spaces away from my girl's empty space. Lying there in a pool of intrigue and anger, I waited. There wouldn't be a confrontation, just observation. I'd be there when she stepped out of her car—and, perhaps, set eyes on the shoes of the man my woman dared bring home.

Problem was, I fell asleep. The emotional adrenaline took its toll, and in the name of love, I fell asleep under the car. Must have been down there for about forty-five minutes. As I said, it was engine coolant that revived me; startling was that sudden drip on my neck. But I'd napped through the event. My girlfriend's car now sat there, empty. So was I. I needed to know the truth.

I looked up at the window of her second-floor apartment. It was dark, even though her car's engine was still warm. She kept an extra key under her front doormat. I'd sneak in undetected and, one way or the other, free my soul.

Under the cloak of darkness, on hands and knees, I made my way through the living room and headed down the short hallway to her bedroom I could smell the faint aroma of perfume and alcohol.

Then I heard something that took my breath away: my girlfriend's voice, murmuring something just above a whisper in a soothing, appreciative tone. She wasn't on the phone; through the open door of her bedroom, in the glow of a night-light I could see it sitting there on the floor next to her bed. I couldn't make out much else, though.

I propped myself up against the wall, reeking of hurt and motor oil, my heart racing so fast that I thought I might keel over. I'd given this woman the best six months of my life and this was the thanks I got.

Singer Ray Parker, Jr., not exactly king of the low-down dirty blues, wrote a rather poignant lyric about coming home early from work, opening up the door and getting your feelings hurt. Different scenario here, but same aching result.

Jive chick never whispered sweet nothings to me at night. To hell with my pride—most of which I'd dis-carded under that Buick, anyway—I had to know what was being said. Composing myself, on all fours I continued my sojourn toward the truth. I reached her bedroom door in time to hear: ". . . and forgive us our trespasses, as we forgive those who trespass against us. Lead us not into temptation; but deliver us from evil. . . ." My girlfriend, here alone, before succumbing to a rum and Coke–induced slumber, was saying her prayers.

It was tough getting out of that apartment—I felt about this tall and couldn't reach the doorknob. Back outside, relief quickly deteriorated into shame.

However, determined to find something amiss, after catching my breath I began to sicken myself with more irrational thoughts: Perhaps she dropped him off at his place before coming home. Hey, maybe she'd skipped the bar and her girlfriends altogether and had spent the evening with him. Whoever he was.

That is how the green-eyed monster called jealousy works. Insecurity's henchman, jealousy creates maddening ideas in your head and nibbles at your very soul with anger and mistrust.

It's all fear. Fear of not being enough of something; fear of being shunned simply for being you. Along with ignorance, fear created racism and prejudice and guns and nuclear bombs and cold war and intercontinental ballistic missiles and the Great Wall of China. For some, it might be difficult to connect industrial-sized fear with accusing a mate of tipping around, but those apples all fall from the same tree.

If you search for something long and hard enough, one way or another, you're going to discover something. Just be prepared for what you find. That night, I found everything I wasn't looking for, in a place I never expected to find it. None of it had anything to do with her and everything to do with me.

No, I never told her.

NETTA'S
LIBERATING SLEEP

I'M NOT BIG ON FLYING. The seating arrangements are cramped and the food is lousy. Yet I'd schlep all the way to the Caribbean to be with Netta.

I met the mocha-skinned beauty in the mid nineties one balmy summer night at the club Paradise 24. She was in Los Angeles while on holiday from the tiny island she called home. Soon, our intense infatuation had me, age thirty-five, spending L.A. winters on the island and Netta, a year younger, joining me in L.A. during summers.

When I'd get to the island, it was always the same: Our first week together would be heaven; the second week a delight. Third week, turbulence. A great day could erupt into emotional chaos at a moment's notice, sparked by a simple question regarding apples or what time *The Simpsons* came on. And the storm could end as abruptly as it began. Netta was a sweet, giving young woman; she was creative and a dreamer. But one day, while walking through a parking lot in the city, I swear I didn't see Netta's reflection in the windows of the cars we passed. Sometimes, being with her was like venturing into a minefield. Proceed with caution.

But when night came, she'd slip into the deepest slumber and the emotional chess game evaporated. Netta would become the gentle soul who initially captivated me, and I'd remember why I spent a small fortune on phone calls and dispatched long, melancholy faxes.

Asleep, all of us revert to a purity of heart that is elusive while we are conscious. We let everything go and surrender to inherent equanimity. At our spirit's core, we are all placid and untainted. Even the most notorious criminal is innocent while he sleeps. If you ever find yourself struggling to forgive someone, observe her sleeping. Scrutinize long enough and you can almost see her wearing a tiara in that school play, or him, completely contented, in a lopsided cowboy hat, clutching an ice cream cone, the contents of which drip along his tiny knuckles.

More than once, I've awakened to find the woman with whom I was currently sharing my life intently gazing at me, possibly pondering why more of what she signed up for hadn't revealed itself during waking hours.

But Netta's sleep was unusual. She'd fall deep and disturbingly still, as if she'd left her body. You couldn't wake her. Her older brother, Jonathan, joked that he'd rather nudge a tiger at siesta than wake his younger sister. Even Netta's mother dutifully advised me never to rouse her sleeping daughter. One time Netta fell asleep on the couch in front of the TV and couldn't be wakened. I went to lift her and unconsciously, she began to flail as if fighting for her life. I put a blanket over her and turned off the TV.

I knew not to wake Netta. And, whether her brother knew the reason, or whether her mother would ever admit it, I also learned why.

The answer confronted me in the wee morning hours, when I mischievously attempted to coax her out of sleep into lovemaking. After spurning my affections, to my quiet shock Netta finally mumbled, "Please, Papa . . . please, don't."

That night after dinner, I diplomatically presented her utterance. She angrily denied it before tearfully admitting that until his death from cancer, her father physically treated his daughter as if she were his wife. At night, she'd awaken to his sinister, wandering hands and whispers, and his weight upon her.

Her mother initially said it never happened, then conceded it might have but disavowed any knowledge of it at the time. Regardless, Netta's sorrowful revelation explained her sound slumber. Sleep served as her refuge, not only as a child, but from the torturous emotional agony that remained, as an adult.

Once again, my Caribbean winter had come to an end. This time, though, so had Netta and I. Neither of us could admit it as we tightly embraced in her kitchen earlier, but we knew our wildly dysfunctional long-distance relationship simply could not withstand our geographical circumstances. Most regrettably, we couldn't get past the pain. I was the enemy one day, her savior the next. I'd give up; she'd be hopeful. The next week we'd trade places. I felt helpless to soothe her soul.

We didn't say much on the way to the airport, but our tears at gate 24 spoke volumes of a love lost. Once situated in my seat on the flight, I peered out the window to see Netta's smiling, tearstained face. It was pressed against the tinted airport terminal glass, amusing passengers and me with her funny faces.

The plane began to move, and Netta's horseplay instantly ceased.

Anxiously, she followed us along the tarmac as far as the airport's windowed corridor would allow her. Mighty jet engines began to roar, and many years later the vision that lingers is one of her hands on the window, framing an anguished smile and longing eyes, unwittingly presenting a desperate portrait that begged freedom. As the businessman to my right offered up a tissue, I wished for Netta the same solace in her troubled life that she found in her sleep.

FOR THE
LOVE OF JOY

IT'S ALL IN THE SHOULDERS," she instructed me through her mischievous laughter. At a music festival in Rancho Park, members of a modern dance troupe had invited the audience to join them onstage for the final number. I pulled away like a child being coerced into giving some sugar to his mustached grandmother, but my reaction wasn't quick enough. She had me up there, making a fool of myself, to the amusement of a couple hundred onlookers.

But then, that was Joy, forever pushing my envelope

of personal control and comfort. It was that way from the day I walked into the mall pharmacy to buy triple-A batteries. She flirted from behind the cash register with those big brown Bambi eyes, daring me to reciprocate. I don't always possess the courage to respond to overtures when they are made, but I figured if I survived her hearty laughter at the denial of my Visa card, then I could risk offering her some ice cream during her next break. Thankfully, she obliged, and a couple scoops down Rocky Road set me on the Freeway of Love.

I believe a name sometimes can dictate personality at birth. A perpetual smile adorning her round face, Joy seldom appeared not to enjoy life. Distinctively, beautifully and charmingly Ethiopian, Joy came to Southern California to attend the premed program at UCLA while living with her two older brothers

I was especially drawn to the prideful way in which she carried herself. It was a characteristic I'd noticed in many Africans, particularly Ethiopians—a quiet pride historically perceived by American blacks as arrogance.

Joy, whose mother and father were both doctors back home in Addis Ababa, was anything but arrogant. However, at just nineteen she seemed quite clear of her place in the world. When flashing red lights appeared in my rearview mirror one evening on our way home from dinner and a movie in Westwood, Joy kept silent in the passenger seat as the police officer, apparently stopping us for the dubious infraction of DWB (Driving While Black), cordially made insulting inquiries without provocation ("Is this your car?" "What is your business on this side of town at this hour?" "Are there any drugs or weapons in this car?" etc.).

When he finished, to the surprise of the cop and to my stark terror, Joy gave him a piece of her mind. Later, when I angrily told her that she could have gotten us arrested or worse, she humbled me by saying the worse occurred when we sat and allowed ourselves to be addressed so disrespectfully.

I'm sure impressing Joy was the primary reason I broke my rule about not mixing business with pleasure and asked her to accompany me to a lavish lunchtime press conference for the Bee Gees.

As a twenty-three-year-old earning my music journalist stripes for the fledgling *Soul Newspaper*, I hadn't covered many events of the magnitude of this hype fest. The lobby of the Beverly Hilton, bustling with the tanned and beautiful, resembled a scene out of a Hollywood novel.

Uniformed bellboys, paging presumably important people to important phone calls, navigated the traffic by jingling a bell and carrying signs with the person's name written on it, just like in old black-and-white movies.

While Joy was giddy, I worked to conceal my sudden intimidation with the whole thing.

We were ushered by a record-company publicist into a ballroom filled with tables of journalists and photographers. The guests at our table managed to look down their noses at us from their seats. A stringer from Reuters remarked she'd never heard of the publication I represented; the gabbing woman from *Newsweek* and guy from *Rolling Stone* never looked up. When the freelancer from *Playboy* gingerly inquired why a black writer would cover the Bee Gees, an annoyed Joy excused herself to the ladies' room.

I sat in isolated silence, feeling completely inadequate and pondering simply slipping out before the festivities began, when the bellboy strode through, jingling his bell for yet another important person. My heart nearly stopped when, this time, I realized the name scribbled on his sign was mine. Nervously, I flagged him down and he brought me a phone. All activity at my table ceased as I said hello.

"Do you know you are the most happening person at your table?" Joy chirped through the receiver.

"You think so?"

"I'm *sure* of it," she said. "They are phony people, baby, all of them. And the *Playboy* guy has body odor."

"Yeah, I know."

"You're important, and you'd better start *being* the part. A lot of people would love to be in your shoes. And I am happy to know the man wearing them." She had me blushing.

"Where did you come from? Where are you now?"

"Ethiopia . . . in the rest room. Now straighten up and act like you're talking to Barry Gordy."

"Berry. His name is Berry Gordy." The table moved in closer.

"See? You know your stuff."

It was funny how quickly something as superficial as a phone call had upped my stock at the table. But suddenly, these people didn't matter. And as much as I dug some of their early stuff, neither did the Bee Gees. Thanks to age-old wisdom from a nineteen-year-old, I simply wanted to get out and bask in the glow of being me. Nonetheless, I felt a bit uncomfortable—embarrassed that I was so oblivious to what Joy already seemed to know so well.

In the four months that followed, Joy and I began to find our groove as a couple. Then one day she tearfully informed me of abrupt plans to return to her homeland to help out at her father's practice. It was a rough last two weeks. After she got back home, a steady stream of loving letters and cards between L.A. and Addis Ababa followed. After waiting almost six months for my last card to be answered, I finally phoned one of Joy's Stateside brothers to get the scoop. Had his sister become consumed by university studies? a serious new courtship? marriage?

He was silent for a moment, sighed heavily and then explained: While walking to their parents' home one afternoon, Joy came upon a burning storefront. She struggled in and out of the place twice, rescuing an elderly man and a little girl; she entered a third time to retrieve a dog, but didn't come back out. Speechless, I held the phone as Joy's brother began to wail as if he'd just been given the news. Finally, her other brother took the receiver, apologized and hung up.

In tears, I slumped on my beat-up plaid couch, cursing an idealistic young girl's selflessness. But then, that was Joy's way, constantly pushing the envelope of love of self and others.

JUST LIKE A FATHER

MANY MEN REFUSE to date women with children. It cramps their style. Single men are accustomed to a certain physical and emotional availability when it comes to the women they see, and children of most any age hamper the hookup.

There are domestic politics: When does the man she is seeing meet the children? This summit usually insinuates something serious. And it's tricky—if the child becomes comfortable with the man, then the child might become attached to the man and the idea of their being a family unit. If that vision doesn't materialize, then the child has to get past all the possibilities that such a relationship presents, just like the parent.

Single mothers often contend with men viewing them as easy to get into bed—as if the time spent raising her family makes her so lonely that she cannot afford to be particular.

Of course, you can't discuss the rite of single-parent dating without the infamous Baby Daddy Drama. God help the man involved with the single mom whose ex uses the child they've created together to make her life miserable.

Working to avoid all the dating pitfalls is enough to make a single mother simply give up on finding happiness with a man. Many reason that the best thing for themselves and their babies is to raise them alone.

Thus, by the time the man who is sincerely willing to get to know her comes along, she is probably more wary than hopeful.

Men emotionally open to the possibilities are aware of the special opportunities within a single-parent family. Here you are, interested in this woman, and these little ones are her creation. They look like her, walk like her, have her mannerisms. Through them, you have yet another chance to experience her.

And though few men know or admit this, he can find himself— his heart and a precious part of life—in a family he didn't create.

I actually found a family before I knew I'd even want one.

I was in my mid-twenties when I met Sosha's mother. I noticed her more than once at a popular after-work cocktail spot before finding the nerve to make conversation. She was single, free from a mostly stormy union that produced the light of her life, a two-year-old daughter. I've always liked children; I think being one once has something to do with it. However, I didn't think much about her daughter until, after meeting for several Fridays at the cocktail spot, one Saturday evening she invited me to her home. That's where I met Sosha.

Sporting sandy curly hair, deep dimples and pajamas, Sosha was about to be put to bed when she was instructed to say hello. That bright smile, enchanting eyes and the way she immediately took to me quickly captured my heart. So did her mom. After just six months of spending all our free time together, it was decided I'd move in.

Living with a woman who has a child can be a delicate undertaking. For one thing, I wasn't sure what Sosha would call me. I wasn't biological Dad, and being "Uncle" to anyone not blood always had an icky connotation for me. It was the girl's mother, of course, who had the monumental task of raising Sosha—cooking for her; nursing her through a lifetime of colds and other childhood maladies; living through braces and new math and life lessons that produce decent human beings.

At first, Sosha and I played together, but I stood idly by while her mother did the parenting. However, a man really hasn't lived until he experiences the faith bestowed him by a woman who trusts him with her child, and my responsibilities began with my reading some nights to Sosha her favorite Golden Book as she sat on my knee. In about a month I was allowed to bathe her, making sure she didn't fall in the toilet as she learned to potty on her own. On Saturday mornings after breakfast I'd give Mommy a break by walking Sosha to the park. Like most toddlers, Sosha couldn't keep her hands off the stereo knobs. She wailed after I swatted her little hand, marking a defining moment on whether I'd be allowed to discipline her or not. Her mother decided that I could, sparingly, but I didn't need to. Sosha learned her lesson the first time.

She doesn't remember the occasional Saturday when

she accompanied me to my office and giggled uncontrollably as she danced to the Police's "Don't Stand So Close to Me," but she did.

After more than two years together, Sosha's mother and I broke up. The demands of my fledgling career as a music journalist—the networking and late-night glad-handing—seemed like so much California dreaming to my sensible bookkeeper lover. Young Sosha couldn't comprehend why I was no longer around, but in a year's time, when her mother and I buried our anger, I was encouraged to visit Sosha, like a lazy actor whose stunt man did all the tough stuff, to enjoy the result of someone else's toil. From then on, I watched from just out of arm's reach as the little girl with the enchanting eyes and bright smile grew up.

When she went to the prom—or whatever that thing was—I proudly played chauffeur and bodyguard, keeping an eye on her big, handsome date through the rearview mirror. When she went off to college, I sat her down and told her to understand that young men sometimes lie. I privately wept when a year later she said I was right. Trading e-mails with her from Italy while she studied there tickled me. And though I personally supplied very little fertilizer, to see the intelligent rose that blossomed from a two-year-old seed into an attractive, loving, respectful, ambitious yet down-to-earth and just a little naive twenty-something young woman has my chest out to there.

Had I not been open to dating a single woman who happened to have a child, I would not have enjoyed one of my life's premium experiences.

Just-Like-a-Father cards on Father's Day melt me like butter in the sun.

BLACK STALLION
IN THE HOUSE

WELL, YOU'RE EARLY. That's a change."

In 1990, during the second week of an Australian summer vacation, I was riding the evening train from the tiny suburban town of St. Mary's, where I was staying with friends.

I was headed into Sydney for a taste of nightlife, when several miles before my destination, on pure inquisitive impulse, I decided to disembark.

I walked into a pub in which I'd never been, in a small, lily-white blue-collar town I didn't know existed until I stepped into it. Yet the weather-beaten, balding man behind the bar was telling me that I was "early." For "a change." I figured this was how they greeted strangers in these parts.

I nursed a Guinness for almost half an hour as I took in the sights and sounds of Friday night in Smallville: The dining room to my right was half full with regular-looking couples and families in Bermuda shorts, T-shirts and jeans, Top-Siders and mountain boots, all partaking in a hearty menu of shepherd's pie, steak and potatoes and oversized hamburgers.

Meanwhile, the barroom where I sat was filled with lanky, boisterous soccer fans yelling at a television hanging from the wall. Just beyond the barroom, farther to my left, was the partially open doorway to a banquet room.

While on my way to the men's room, I glimpsed in that banquet room the makings of what looked to be a private party. A version of the soul classic "When Something Is Wrong with My Baby" blared from the DJ's speakers while a jovial aggregation of women, ranging from their mid-thirties to senior citizenry, drank, played darts and cards, and perused a buffet table.

When I came out of the men's room, I ran into a spry, elderly woman who took one look at me, flashed an inebriated grin and issued a decidedly sexy, "Well, hel-*low* there!" before heading back into the private room.

A bartender who says I'm "early" tonight; a grandma who greets me as if she knows me, or wants to. I wondered what was in Smallville's water system.

I asked for another round.

"Oh, taking our time tonight, are we?" the bartender replied, adding just a pinch of sarcasm to my second glass of Guinness. "It's probably just as well," he continued. "Let 'em get good and sauced, since the cheap wenches usually up and leave right afterward."

Being in the Twilight Zone is particularly tormenting if you're the only one who doesn't know the plot. I'd had enough.

"Sir, what is your name?" I asked.

"I'm Josh."

"Forgive me, Josh, but . . . just what are you talking about?"

Visibly annoyed, he put down a bottle of whiskey and moved closer. "I'm talkin' 'bout you comin' in early," he said sternly, but keeping his voice down, "and then sittin' here swiggin' like you're on holiday."

He reached under the counter and, with a fair amount of frustration driving the action, slapped a flyer down on the bar in front of me. "I don't know about you, but where I'm from, six o'clock means six o'clock," he said, pointing to blue Magic Marker scribble that said SIX and $150.00.

He walked off to prepare drinks for the impatient barmaid at the other end, and I turned the flyer around to read: BLACK STALLION ENTERTAINMENT PRESENTS BLACK MALE DANCERS & STRIPPERS. PRIVATE PARTIES, SPECIAL FUNCTIONS. SINGLE OR ENSEMBLE PERFORMANCES. PROFESSIONAL. REASONABLE RATES. SATISFACTION GUARANTEED. Next to the words "Black Stallion" was a logo—the faceless silhouette of a hunky black, muscular body.

"Business is business," said Josh, back at my end of the bar. "You guys agreed to four Fridays at six on the dot, but you're the only one of these brown yanks who gets here on time—and now you're 'bout to be late too, sittin' here downing drinks."

Turned out, that banquet room was hosting an office party of employees from a petroleum company, and Josh assumed I was the commissioned entertainment. The very idea was laughable. For most of my life I've been shy about my body. I'm the skinny guy whose gangly frame could use some weight.

Boys would use their thumb and middle finger to measure the size of my wrist and bust up in mocking laughter.

I remember sending off for these edible calorie tablets (a precursor to today's protein powders), which guaranteed to pack pounds onto the meager frame of any pimply faced kid gullible enough to order it. Hawking it in the novelty section of comic books, among ads for X-ray glasses and whoopee cushions, was an industrious move; by the time you read through fifteen or so pages of ass-whupping by Batman or Justice League of America, you were ready to try anything offering you a leg up in life. I used to gag trying to keep the horrid tasting stuff down.

It figured that the pub would employ strippers, though; in Australia, exotic dancing is big business, and merchants consider it a viable remedy to most immediate fiscal woes. If damn near any small business has a day in the week when commerce is down, out goes a banner touting an exotic-dancing schedule.

I even ran into a sister on vacation from the States who said what the hell and earned some extra cash stripping. A school teacher in D.C., she shook her groove thang Down Under as "Mocha Passion."

I looked up from the flyer and pondered the private party. Just the thought of standing in front of anyone—especially women—and deliberately bringing attention to my body made me perspire. Then again, no one in that room knew me; no one in this town knew me. I was more than seven thousand miles away from America. As far as I was concerned, there wasn't a negative consequence attached whatsoever.

Fuck it—tonight I'd be the Black Stallion.

"Gimme a shot of Cuervo Gold so I can do this and get on outta here," I said, feigning the wearied yawn of a veteran sex symbol. I tossed back the tequila and told the bartender I'd return in a second, walked out the front door around to the parking lot out back, got on the ground between two cars and started doing push-ups. A couple en route to their car came out just in time to catch me agonizing through the last two. "I'm the entertainment tonight," I said, getting to my feet.

"It's a free world, mate," the man mumbled, pulling his puzzled-looking date just a little closer as they went by.

I walked back into the bar feeling, whether or not I actually looked any different, all puffed up. Josh introduced me to the DJ from the private room.

"Give him your music, mate," he said.

"What music?" I asked.

"You guys usually bring your own music. You don't have music?"

"Oh . . . oh shit. I forgot to bring my music," I said, playing along. "What do you have," I asked, turning to the DJ.

"Rock—Stones, Rod Stewart. Dance stuff, too."

That wasn't going to get it. In my experience of watching strippers, I'd seen girls without the typical curves turn a place out with stage technique and sheer heart. This wasn't going to be about a hulking body; I needed to be able to move to some good music. "You got any R&B?"

He returned with the only R&B under the roof, a CD compilation of old-school soul and funk hits. "I'm gonna come out with this one," I instructed, pointing to Aretha Franklin's "Rock Steady," "and after that, play this one"—the Isley Brothers' "It's Your Thing." "But let's start now." If I didn't do this immediately, I was going to chicken out. Furthermore, my chest was shrinking.

Josh led me through the pub's kitchen to a service door that I'd walk out of to face my audience.

Just before the bartender brought me back there, I was all right about this. Alas, in the intoxicated seconds that I waited for my cue, I suddenly felt as if I might hyperventilate. I kept it together by breathing deeply and reminding myself where I was. *Man, you crossed the international date line to get here. You don't know any of these people. After tonight, they'll never see you again.*

Still, I trembled when I heard the gospel-tinged organ intro to "Rock Steady." I couldn't believe I was doing this. "ALLLL RIGHT ladies," announced the DJ. "This is the moment you've been waiting for! Direct from the good ol' USA—It's the BIG, BROWN BLACK STALLION!!"

There was a smattering of hooting, yelping and clapping as I pushed myself through the door, and in the nanosecond before I did, something happened: I became someone else. Gregarious. Aggressive. Sexy? As they say in the 'hood back home, I had to come outta my ass.

"What's happenin', ladies?" I shouted, clapping my hands to the beat and strutting to the front of the room. "Y'all ready to party?" If I was going to survive out here, first thing I was going to have to do was get them involved. "I asked you a question—are y'all ready to PARTY! !" I motioned for them to clap with me on the two and the four, as opposed to the hootenanny one and three that white folks the world over seem to fall into during even the funkiest grooves. They actually found the rhythm, and I began to do what I've heard a million performers say they do with an audience—work off the crowd's energy.

I kept moving. They didn't care what I did, as long as it was masculine and sexy. And "black." These women had paid to experience the mighty, sculpted physique and exaggerated sexuality that is the stereotypical epitome of a black man. That man didn't show up tonight, and so there was I.

That's where that tequila came in, allowing me to smile confidently and fearlessly imagine I was doing my thing in the privacy of my bathroom mirror. *Aww, shhhh-hucks, Stevie. You got 'em, baby. Keep movin'. You big, baby.*

Big and Black . . . Aretha's track was heaving and proud: ". . . Rock steady, rock steady, baby. . . ."

"Who wants to deal with all this tonight?" I challenged, shouting over the Queen of Soul.

"All what?" someone called back from the corner.

That's okay, Stevie. Keep movin'. Keeeep movin'.

Shit, what do I do now? I can't let the whole song play without taking off something. I began to unbutton my shirt.

"Now you're gettin' down to business, hon," said a voice.

I came out of that shirt, slowly; I figured if I took enough time, someone might stick his head in the place and yell "fire"; or lightning might strike the building; or perhaps a contained, survivable nuclear attack would strike New South Wales. Something had to happen to deliver me from the moment.

Alas, none of those things happened, and when the shirt came off, it was as if all of Australia had just been disappointed. Someone, presumably the same ungrateful old bitty whom a minute ago rudely questioned the goods, muttered something about a brown pigeon instead of a Black Stallion. Indeed, the world probably doesn't know an audience more cruel than a group of horny, middle-aged white women who suddenly ascertain their Negro beefcake to be little more than rib ends.

I had to generate some excitement. They were still clapping to the music, but probably out of charity and for the fact that they were here and half drunk and not home parked in front of the TV. I had the presence of mind to scan the room and locate my number one fan— the grandma who'd given me the big hello earlier in the evening.

I hustled on over and did what performers dying on the vine do—play to the person who digs them. I began to seductively gyrate in front of the old lady, and she played right along, rising in delight from her chair to gyrate with me. The room loved it, getting more of a kick out of her than me, perhaps, but I didn't care.

Once rekindling some interest, I moved back to the front of the room. I couldn't figure out why the DJ wasn't playing the Isley Brothers—instead, segueing into Rod Stewart's "Do Ya Think I'm Sexy"; I was too busy trying to look like I knew what I was doing. I began to unbuckle my belt and the room suddenly roared, as if this were what they'd been waiting for, and big Steve was about to give it to them.

Then I noticed they weren't looking at me.

The ladies were transfixed on what was just behind me: About six foot three and two hundred and something pounds of black, chiseled muscular mass, he was a Mack truck masquerading as a human being. The real Black

Stallion had arrived. Already out of his shirt, he was looking at me playfully, as if challenging me to a strip-off.

I slowly danced backward, moved up next to him and
yelled over the music, "MAN, WHAT TOOK YOU SO
FUCKING LONG?" He just laughed and shook my hand
before I backed myself through the kitchen door, met by
an irate Josh. "You impostor. If you think I'm going to
pay you, then you're out of your frickin' mind."

"Let me tell you something," I replied as I put an arm
into my shirt. "For what just happened to me out there,
I ought to pay you. Now calm down and come pour me
another Guinness."

At the bar I could hear squeals and screams emanat-
ing from the private room; that brother was giving them
their fantasy's worth. When he finished, he collected his
fee from Josh, ordered himself a drink and joined me.

He said he'd first come Down Under while on tour in
the navy, fell in love with the place and ended up staying. Initially, exotic dancing was an amusing way for him
to make some extra cash, but soon it evolved into a full-
time business.

"Hey, I could use you," he said, half serious. "A lot of
chicks like skinny dudes. We'd bill you as The Thin
Man." I graciously declined.

The private party began filing out, and the grandma I
danced with came over. "I was pullin' for you, kiddo,"

she said with a consoling wink. "Had you come out of those trousers, I think we might have won 'em over."

Entertainers say that it sometimes takes them hours to come down from the adrenaline-induced high after a performance. I can vouch for this; I could have run into town alongside the train that finally took me into Sydney.

On board, I sat abuzz, drunk on gumption I didn't know I owned, my face smeared with the silly half grin of a mischievous kid keeping a juicy secret.

In the future, I'd wrestle with self-doubt again and again. However, my uneasy triumph that night in a pub on the other side of the world started a personal fire I'd never allow to die. What to do for an encore? When I got back to the States, perhaps I'd run for president.

A club called The Tunnel in Sydney's Darling Harbor was just beginning to jump at a quarter to eleven when I slid past the doorman and into an international throng of designer label–clad Beautiful People. Some appeared to look condescendingly on my Gap uniform of white button-down long-sleeve shirt and crisp khakis, but I could only smile, for these mild-mannered duds served me well in concealing my true, secret identity: Watch out, baby. Black Stallion is in the house.

A WOMAN'S GOTTA HAVE IT

IT WASN'T THAT TARA was dressed provocatively. In the three months we'd been going out, she'd certainly dressed sexier. In fact, the turquoise sarong with the pink flower print she was wearing effectively concealed all the goods.

But as I tagged along behind her at the Pasadena flea market, carrying her purchases, the subtle dance of those flowers on her backside, driven by the systematic movement of Tara's firm buttocks, beckoned me all afternoon.

We'd gotten just inside her apartment when, without saying a word, I grabbed her thick head of hair, pulled her into me and kissed her hard as I undid that damned sarong. It dropped to the living room floor and I pulled her down on top of it.

The buttons flew as I ripped apart the front of the cotton blouse to reveal her small, beautiful breasts. I licked and sucked hungrily as Tara deliriously mumbled something about either the sarong or her carpet. In a few seconds I felt her body go limp and surrender.

I handled her as if she were my property and told her as much, and as she writhed and moaned with her eyes closed, I could see that she loved every syllable. I continued to kiss her as I kept a tight knot of her hair in my right hand and roughly caressed her inner thighs with my left. Indeed, it was my hand that first bought her to the brink and eventually pushed her over the top.

Afterward we lay on our backs like exhausted runners who'd crossed a finish line.

"If you had broken the martini glasses I just brought, I'd have cut you," Tara joked before gazing up at the ceiling light fixture and turning introspective. "Do you know how long I've been wanting what we just did?"

I replied with something clichéd like "If you're satisfied, I'm satisfied." However, as she thanked me, I was secretly thanking the unlikely cohort in our sexual escapade: her ex-boyfriend.

You see, one evening on the phone shortly after our first date several weeks before, Tara and I talked about sex. Casually but candidly, we discussed what we liked and didn't like. Her initial discomfort gave way to schoolgirl giggles, but eventually we engaged in some explicit adult dialogue about our sexual fantasies and carnal desires, something her ex-boyfriend of two and a half years was never inclined to do. "Anytime I broached the subject of sex with him, he would say 'The act speaks for itself.' " His attitude isn't unlike that of many men and women who, as a result of feeble communication on the subject, often go through much of their lives not getting the sex they fantasize about.

I learned the importance of talking about sex in my early thirties, while having a purely sexual relationship with a twenty-six-year-old yoga instructor. Perhaps it was because we mutually agreed it wasn't a love thing that the sex was so open and without abandon. All I know is that I'd never met a woman so concerned with my enjoyment, and so willing to explain to me with remarkable ease and candor what she liked and how she wanted it done. She once said that life is too short for consenting adults to engage in anything but the kind of sex they dream about.

Miss Yoga said we should also listen to a lover's body. If she moans in fake ecstasy but physically tenses up like an ironing board, she's really saying, "Your ingenious technique down there is making me raw, okay? Stop it."

Yoga Girl's advice notwithstanding, the best lesson available on how to treat a woman comes from legendary soul singer Bobby Womack in the form of his 1972 classic, "A Woman's Gotta Have It." Even if you think you know exactly what you're doing, player, it won't hurt to listen to Womack expound on the bylaws of keeping your woman happy. Indeed, there are the emotional intricacies, but if, as Womack croons, you "give her what she wants when she wants it, how she wants it and every doggone time she feels she needs it," no matter what goes on in the relationship, she is going to think twice about stepping out into a world with a shortage of good men and a surplus of lousy sex.

Short of swinging from a chandelier—or involvement with children, animals or another dude—there isn't much I won't do to please a woman. Even in the twenty-first century, sex in a heterosexual relationship is generally controlled by the man, and the guy willing to discover and participate in his partner's carnal desires can find a special place in a woman's heart. It was my willingness in this area that most appealed to Gloria.

We met at Fox Hills mall, where she was a sales manager at a department store. For about a year we were just friends before pursuing a more intimate relationship. Mild-mannered and sexy in a matronly way, she was one of the few black Republicans I'd ever met. But while she honed conservative social and political views, in bed, Plain Jane was an animal.

One evening after sex, lying in her bed sharing relationship tales, Gloria told me she broke up with a guy who was her "soul mate" but for his penchant for anal sex. I suggested that if she really thought he was her soul mate, then perhaps she might have at least tried it.

"As if you'd do something you really didn't want to do," she responded, sitting up and putting on her glasses.

"Listen, I'll try anything once," I said. "If I don't like it, I won't do it again. But you have to be open, Gloria."

"That's easy to say, when you're doing the gettin' and the woman is doing the givin'."

"I'm just saying that if my soul mate asked me to try something, I'd have to at least be open to the idea. Sex should be an adventure."

Gloria was silent for a second, then rolled over to her night stand, opened the drawer and held up a white plastic battery-powered dildo that looked to be about six inches. "You're telling me *you'd* have something like this put up your ass?"

"In the name of love, yes."

She smiled. "What about in the name of sexual exploration?"

Now, I don't even like a woman's finger up there, let alone a stylized plastic phallic device. But I couldn't preach sexual freedom and awareness to Gloria if I wasn't willing to practice it. I figured what the hell. "In the name of sexual exploration? Sure. I'll try it."

Gloria said the dildo was already clean, but I insisted she head to the bathroom, thoroughly wash her toy and bring back a bottle of rubbing alcohol, with which I swabbed it down with Kleenex. Begrudgingly, I then rolled over on my stomach. Gloria laughed at how generous I was with the K-Y jelly at the gates of the Forbidden Kingdom. Slowly she began penetration.

"Ummmph." She hadn't inserted more than an inch of the thing when I said I'd had enough.

Laughter.

"How does it feel?"

"In a word, intrusive."

"This is what he said he wanted from me every night."

"Well, I don't blame you for breaking up with the cat over this. Take it out."

Gloria responded by nudging the dildo in an inch more. "This not only feels this way in a woman's butt," she said with a steely calm. "A dick can feel this way going in the vagina, too. Men think they can just ram it in—"

"Gloria, stop playing around!"

"Relax, baby," she said sarcastically.

I managed to turn my head around and get a glimpse of Gloria, who straddled my left thigh, her hand firmly in my back. Her face was set in a scary smirk and she glared weirdly. I should mention here that Gloria was not a small woman. At five foot seven, she checked in at a sexy, curvaceous and not-easy-to-toss 150. In this position, a skinny guy like me was clearly at a disadvantage.

"Now you can feel a woman's pain," she said with demonic detachment.

Tactfully, I agreed with her, but I lied. This was distinctively the pain of a straight man—with way too much of a six-inch dildo up his ass, knocking on the door of his prostate. Bobby Womack would never be caught in a spot like this. The open, uninhibited love-meister had no choice but to, as Womack would say, come out of a different bag.

"Woman, get the fuck up off me and get this thing outta my ass!"

Gloria snapped out of her devil-with-a-dildo stance and let me up. We made fun about it later, but the damage was done. I'd killed my rep with her as the Love Man in Control by letting my mouth write a check that my booty hole could not, would not and had no intention of cashing.

That doesn't happen to me very often, though.

There may be guys who are better looking, guys with more money. Men who can still grow hair. However, you won't find a man more committed to his woman's sexual pleasure than me. Her desire is my desire. Her wish is my command.

And none of that five, ten-minute stuff, either. I like to take my time, to savor every exciting level of lovemaking, from kisses and heated foreplay to the sweaty, impassioned crescendo that delivers my lover to the promised land. Thank God I learned firsthand the golden gospel that many men simply refuse to understand: A woman, no matter what she says, has got to have it.

LAST MAN
STANDING

WHEN I NOTICE A MAN is wearing a wedding band on his finger, I know there goes a man who has vowed to share his life with a woman, through sickness and health, good times and bad credit, and he made his decision official by doing what is considered by society to be the apex of commitment: He got married.

These days, I see mankind as divided into two types of men—married and single.

I belong to a small, informal fraternity of male

friends in our forties who have yet to marry. Some of us have lived with women for various periods of time; others have fathered children out of wedlock. Most of us insist we are sincerely open to the concept of marriage; it simply has to be "right."

Depending on the man, "right" might be defined as anything from finding Madame Curie in a supermodel's body to a woman who really knows how to fry chicken.

However, in the eyes of married couples and singles who just want to be married, until we stand with a woman before a preacher, priest, licensed minister or justice of the peace, we will always be known as The Uncommitted.

When asked why I haven't yet married, I know the question is merely a formality. Even if I replied that I've been in a monastery for much of my adult life or that I'd recently awakened from a twenty-year coma, an opinion would have already been formed. To them, I am a man afraid to commit.

The real answer to the question is simple: I've yet to meet a woman with whom I felt I wanted to spend the rest of my life. This may sound like a variation of the weak "I just haven't found her yet," or the clichéd, self-deprecating "Who'd put up with *me*?" but it isn't. I've thought long and hard about it, and this answer is the truth.

In my life, I've been blessed to know some great

women—women any man would be lucky to know—and in all of them I found a measure of fulfillment.

The nurturing Danielle taught me the meaning of love and sex and the difference between the two. Jeannette, a pretty, smart aspiring actress who came along when I was more concerned with building a writing career than getting married, defined patience for me. I could not have found a woman more willing a make a relationship work than Colette, who defied her father's choice of who she should date to see me. As it turned out, toward the end of our live-in relationship, ol' girl had some wild oats to sow.

Honestly, at the time, Lord knows I wasn't the greatest prize these women could hope for, either. I wasn't emotionally mature, nor the most communicative or openly affectionate.

However, most all the women I loved lacked in one area: None of them truly understood me. Despite their interest in me, they never believed that my occasionally stoic way had nothing to do with them. Or that my ability to enjoy my own company didn't diminish my desire to be with them, or that my reluctance to spend extended time with their families didn't mean I didn't like their folks (well, in one instance it did, but just that one).

Of course, through trial and tribulation I've since learned that even the most seemingly perfect union requires communication, mutual respect and a willingness to compromise. And that relationship begins with compatibility.

I have no aversion to commitment. I've simply yet to find all that I want to commit to, and no longer am I afraid to say this for fear of being branded a cop-out. I'm tired of trying to fit a square peg into a round hole. I'm through pursuing women I don't have much in common with, for the sake of being involved.

There are couples who shouldn't be together, regardless of how good they look side by side, how great the sex is or what their combined incomes afford them. Because eventually, it won't be about the sex or the acquired stuff. It's going to be about the fine print the minister recites during the wedding ceremony that sounds like so much blah, blah, blah, but is the foundation of a strong union. Good times aside, marriage is about cleaning up the vomit when the normally capable partner reverts to age five after contracting the flu. Inevitably, marriage is going to be about the depth of your love.

Call me idealistic, but I'll commit when I've found the person who in more ways than one completes me; someone who puts a period at the end of my sentence, who is the gravy on my dressing. Forget thick and thin— I'm talking about someone willing to stick with me through thin and thinner. As one of my single buddies puts it, I don't want to throw the fight, I want to be knocked out. That's what I want. And, after years of going through the motions, knowing what I want has now made my search even more difficult.

Of course I worry. Sometimes when I am alone late at night, I wonder: What if there is no one for me? The prospect of going through some of the best, most important years of life without a partner is frightening. There is nothing sadder, reasoned a member of the fraternity, than an old single player in a rest home, visited by some of the old women he used to play. Worse: being in a marriage that has long fallen into a loveless abyss of boredom, lies and frustration. I know too many married couples living this way.

I'm not going out in either fashion. Please, God, don't let me go out like that.

I know she is out there. The stakes are high, but I'll keep searching. Who knows? I could meet her in a supermarket parking lot. I might run into her at the beach. At church. A mutual friend could introduce us. We could meet on an airplane. However she comes to me, I will know it is her, and I'll get to know her and come to love her. And I'll do something I've never done before. I will commit myself, fully and completely.

I wish she would come on.

MY SECRET VALENTINE

ACCORDING TO LEGEND, the Valentine's Day tradition began in honor of Catholic priest and subsequent saint Valentine, who served during the third century in Rome. When Emperor Claudius II decided that single instead of married men with children should fight the wars, he declared marriage for young men illegal.

Valentine is said to have defied Claudius, performing marriages for young lovers in secret. When he was arrested, it is believed that Valentine, before his death, sent the first "valentine" greeting from prison himself to the admiring daughter of the jailer, signing his final letter, "From Your Valentine." He died on February 14, 269. Since then, Hallmark, florists and confectioners have all made a killing off lovers who express their affection on Love's Holiday.

One of the best things about Valentine's Day is that you can use it to convey feelings of love to someone who doesn't know how you feel about them. So, I've decided to let a very special person in my life know my feelings. It's a bit awkward and certainly embarrassing, because, to be honest, in only the last four years have I truly come to grips with my feelings about this person.

We've known each other for what seems like forever. We came up in the same neighborhood. Went from trikes to bikes together, shared experiences deemed momentous events in young lives. Like the time at the candy counter in TG&Y when a guy tried to bully money from my younger brother Tony—and I found the courage to get busy.

Or later on in life, when Don Minnis borrowed his father's Dodge Satellite so we could see Stevie Wonder and Funkadelic at the Oklahoma City Fairgrounds Arena—and then we slid on the winter ice in the parking lot after the show, nearly wrecking the car. It's not easy for anyone to endure the sudden loss of a loved one, especially a fifteen-year-old boy losing his mother. But my friend was by my side for that, too—a child trying to comfort a child.

My compadre was willing to relive every lusty detail of my first kiss with Shirley Brown, over and over. And over.

I remembered the day Mr. Harris, our high school counselor, called me into his office. It was near the end of my senior year at Douglass High, and Mr. Harris said he had good news and bad news. The good news was that I'd indeed march with my high school class. The bad news was that I'd graduate with a D average. I had to conceal my elation; hell, I didn't expect to make it out at all. We celebrated, against my dear friend's better judgment, by doing what I felt was only proper—ditching out the rest of the school year.

I'm lucky and grateful that my friend accompanied me, kicking and screaming, into adulthood. Was there for my loss of a nuisance called virginity. Together, we celebrated my good choices—we both thought Joy, the sweet girl from Ethiopia, God bless her soul, was marriage material—and the bad: Privately, we knew my angst-filled long-distance romance with Netta simply could not last.

My friend watched me learn responsibility; lends unflinching support as I continue to grasp, still, just what it means to be a man. Taught me how to take a compliment. Held my hand through all situations and predicaments, personal, professional and spiritual.

The biggest thing is, my friend was there when I had to swallow some hard facts about myself. Like the role I myself play in my disappointments, and my failure to be completely honest with who I am in the assessment of my life.

We've grown together. Perhaps this is what allowed me to take our relationship for granted in the first place. Familiarity doesn't always breed contempt. However, sometimes, neglect and contempt are one and the same.

Today, it hurts to think that I once thought my friend wasn't "good" enough for me—that I was often embarrassed to have this person around and wouldn't hide the fact. I showed blatant disrespect, even though my friend's belief in me never faltered. Thank God my friend patiently stuck around until this fool, in his lifelong search for love, finally stumbled upon the truth.

A few years ago, I began to look at this person from every angle: Emotionally. Physically. Spiritually. I came to the conclusion—after all this time, can you believe it?—that with a person like this in my corner, I can probably do just about anything. So now I am way beyond a crush. This is—well, there I go hesitating again—this is . . . *love*. And no longer will I try to hide it.

I won't simply hint and hope my friend "gets it"; nor will I speak my feelings in a halfhearted way. In a blank Valentine's Day card, I will be open and honest and say all that is in my heart. I will verbally tell how I feel, as well.

As you might imagine, I've got much ground to cover. There is a lot of explaining to do, and I have to say it all just right. So please, excuse me while I get to writing that note. Dear Self . . .

ACKNOWLEDGMENTS

WITH LOVE, RESPECT and appreciation I gratefully acknowledge:

The Ivory Family: Marjorie, John, Gerald, Barbara, Anthony, Kevin, Tonda, Debra, John Eric, Karen and Lenny, Frank, Brandon, Marlon and Velia; Jessie, Christine and Jewel Turner; Mary, Clifford, Clifford Jr., Joyce Walker and Don Minnis; Ethel Davis; Betty, Charlotte, Cornelius and Guy Lewis; Ronnie Tredwell and family, Miss Holmes, Bobbie Holmes, Ramona, Bunny, Bryn Bacey, and everyone else from Sixth and High, Oklahoma City.

ACKNOWLEDGMENTS

Cherise Grant, Senior Editor, Simon & Schuster, my elegant taskmaster, who reached out and invited me to write this book, and then insisted, in her intuitive, savvy way, that I really tell the stories. You've made me a better writer in the process, and I appreciate your willingness, your optimism and your vision. This is your book; I only wrote it.

Regina Jones, for giving a kid the life-altering opportunity of a lifetime at *Soul Newspaper;* Bob Jones, for your guidance and friendship; Bobby Holland, for your lifelong camaraderie and the wonderful memories we created together; John McClain for providing Technicolor to a life that just wouldn't be the same without you in it; the indefatigable Gary Taylor, for your love and loyalty; Lee Bailey, without whom this book would not have happened and to whom I am forever grateful; J. Randy Taraborrelli, for your experience-tempered advice, but most of all, for a friendship that just gets better with time. Thank you for guiding me through this. To Denzel Washington, for the single sentence of priceless advice you don't even remember dispensing on a Gulfstream at 30,000 feet; Rachel Litchfield, for selfless dedication and support that is love on another level; my man Rodney Saulsbery, for an endless source of joy and inspiration; brother Herb Trawick, for being the vital part of a perfect 10; comrade Bryan Loren, for the opportunity to witness your tremendous talent ("Wanna do it? If you don't wanna do it, just say you don't wanna do it. . . ."); Vidal Sassoon, for giving our story the sweetest ending ever and to Ronnie Sassoon for being a vital part of the addendum; Drex Heikes at *Los Angeles Times Sunday Magazine* for your view of my work; Marlene Connor Lynch, for invaluable advice and believing early when few others did; Pamela Johnson, for submitting my work to editors without my even knowing it (now, that's love); Tavis Smiley, for your praise and support; Charles Freeman, for your spirit and the great conversations; David Nathan, for your motivating words early in the process; Janine Covney, for encouragement when it meant so much; and Michael Horowitz, for the generosity of your time and ingenuity and showing me a way out.

As usual, thank you, James T. McDonough, for sharing with me The Power.

A special heartfelt thank you to my loyal readers at the Electronic Urban Report (www.eurweb.com), who have given me what every artist dreams of: an audience that responds and encourages. This book was born out of your collective embrace. I am gratified.

To Miss Boehm: for being, without question, one of the best things ever to happen to me.